weightwatchers360°

Simply solo

150 Easy and Delicious Recipes for One

Smoked paprika imparts fire-kissed flavor to this dish.
SMOKY SHRIMP AND ROASTED RED PEPPER WITH LINGUINE, PAGE 60

Simply
solo

A simple, spicy chili that's perfect for a weeknight supper.
EDAMAME–BLACK BEAN CHILI, PAGE 124

ABOUT WEIGHT WATCHERS

Weight Watchers International, Inc. is the world's leading provider of weight-management services, operating globally through a network of company-owned and franchise operations. Weight Watchers holds nearly 45,000 meetings each week worldwide, at which members receive group support and education about healthful eating patterns, behavior modification, and physical activity. Weight-loss and weight-management results vary by individual. We recommend that you attend Weight Watchers meetings to benefit from the supportive environment and follow the comprehensive Weight Watchers program, which includes a food plan, an activity plan, and a behavioral component. **WeightWatchers.com** provides subscription weight-management products, such as eTools and Weight Watchers Mobile, and is the leading internet-based weight-management provider in the world. In addition, Weight Watchers offers a wide range of products, publications (including **Weight Watchers Magazine**, which is available on newsstands and in Weight Watchers meeting rooms), and programs for people interested in weight loss and control. For the Weight Watchers meeting nearest you, call **1-800-651-6000**. For information about bringing Weight Watchers to your workplace, call **1-800-8AT-WORK**.

Weight Watchers Publishing Group

VP, Editorial Director Nancy Gagliardi
Creative Director Ed Melnitsky
Photo Director Deborah Hardt
Managing Editor Diane Pavia
Assistant Editor Katerina Gkionis
Food Editor Eileen Runyan
Editor Jackie Mills, R.D.
Nutrition Consultant Jacqueline Kroon, M.S., R.D.
Recipe Developers Terry Grieco Kenny, Maureen Luchejko,
Paul Piccuito, Carol Prager, Mark Scarbrough, and Bruce Weinstein
Production Manager Alan Biederman
Photographer Iain Bagwell
Food Stylist Toni Brogan
Prop Stylist Penelope Bouklas
Art Director Gary Tooth, Empire Design Studio
Designer Elizabeth Stem

SKU #11987
Printed in the USA

Front cover: Salmon and Swiss Chard with Tomato-Fennel Salsa, page 59.
Back cover: Buffalo-Blue Cheese Chicken Sliders, page 12; Shrimp Posole,
page 121; Strawberries and Cream Tartlets, page 143.

CONTENTS

Pickled ginger gives the salad a burst of flavor.
PAN-SEARED COD WITH ASIAN CUCUMBER SALAD, PAGE 116

ABOUT OUR RECIPES

While losing weight isn't only about what you eat, Weight Watchers realizes the critical role it plays in your success and overall good health. That's why our philosophy is to offer great-tasting, easy recipes that are nutritious as well as delicious. We make every attempt to use wholesome ingredients and to ensure that our recipes fall within the recommendations of the U.S. Dietary Guidelines for Americans for a diet that promotes health and reduces the risk for disease. If you have special dietary needs, consult with your health-care professional for advice on a diet that is best for you, then adapt these recipes to meet your specific nutritional needs.

To achieve these good-health goals and get the maximum satisfaction from the foods you eat, we suggest you keep the following information in mind while preparing our recipes:

WEIGHT WATCHERS 360° AND GOOD NUTRITION

▶ Recipes in this book have been developed for Weight Watchers members who are following Weight Watchers 360°. *PointsPlus*® values are given for each recipe. They're assigned based on the amount of protein, carbohydrates, fat, and fiber contained in a single serving of a recipe.

▶ Recipes include approximate nutritional information: they are analyzed for Calories (Cal), Total Fat, Saturated Fat (Sat Fat), Trans Fat, Cholesterol (Chol), Sodium (Sod), Carbohydrates (Carb), Sugar, Dietary Fiber (Fib), Protein (Prot), and Calcium (Calc). The nutritional values are calculated by registered dietitians, using nutrition analysis software.

▶ Substitutions made to the ingredients will alter the per-serving nutritional information and may affect the *PointsPlus* value.

▶ Our recipes meet Weight Watchers Good Health Guidelines for eating lean proteins and fiber-rich whole grains and for having at least five servings of vegetables and fruits and two servings of low-fat or fat-free dairy products a day, while limiting your intake of saturated fat, sugar, and sodium.

▶ Health agencies recommend limiting sodium intake. To stay in line with this recommendation, we keep sodium levels in our recipes reasonably low; to boost flavor, we often include fresh herbs or a squeeze of citrus instead of salt. If you don't have to restrict your sodium, feel free to add a touch more salt as desired.

▶ In the recipes, a green triangle (▲) indicates Weight Watchers® Power Foods.

▶ STAY ON TRACK suggestions have a *PointsPlus* value of *0* unless otherwise stated.

▶ Recipes that work with the Simply Filling technique are listed on page 200. Find more details about this technique at your meeting.

▶ For information about the science behind lasting weight loss and more, please visit **Weight-Watchers.com/science.**

CALCULATIONS NOT WHAT YOU EXPECTED?

▶ You might expect some of the *PointsPlus* values in this book to be lower when some of the foods they're made from, such as fruits and vegetables, have no *PointsPlus* values. Most fruits and veggies have no *PointsPlus* values when served as a snack or part of a meal, like a cup of berries with a sandwich. But if these foods are part of a recipe, their fiber and nutrient content are incorporated into the recipe calculations. These nutrients can affect the *PointsPlus* value.

▶ Alcohol is included in our *PointsPlus* calculations. Because alcohol information is generally not included on nutrition labels, it's not an option to include when using the hand calculator or the online calculator. But since we include alcohol information that we get from our nutritionists, you might notice discrepancies between the *PointsPlus* values you see in our recipes, and the values you get using the calculator. The *PointsPlus* values listed for our recipes are the most accurate values.

SHOPPING FOR INGREDIENTS

As you learn to eat healthier and add more Weight Watchers Power Foods to your meals, remember these tips for choosing foods wisely:

Lean Meats and Poultry Purchase lean meats and poultry, and trim them of all visible fat before cooking. When poultry is cooked with the skin on, we recommend removing the skin before eating. Nutritional information for recipes that include meat, poultry, and fish is based on cooked, skinless boneless portions (unless otherwise stated), with the fat trimmed.

Seafood Whenever possible, our recipes call for seafood that is sustainable and deemed the most healthful for human consumption so that your choice of seafood is not only good for the oceans but also good for you. For more information about the best seafood choices and to download a pocket guide, go to environmentaldefensefund.org or montereybayaquarium.org. For information about mercury and seafood go to weightwatchers.com.

Produce For best flavor, maximum nutrient content, and the lowest prices, buy fresh local produce, such as vegetables, leafy greens, and fruits, in season. Rinse them thoroughly before using, and keep a supply of cut-up vegetables and fruits in your refrigerator for convenient healthy snacks.

Whole Grains Explore your market for whole-grain products such as whole wheat and whole-grain breads and pastas, brown rice, bulgur, barley, cornmeal, whole wheat couscous, oats, and quinoa to enjoy with your meals.

PREPARATION AND MEASURING

Read the Recipe Take a couple of minutes to read through the ingredients and directions before you start to prepare a recipe. This will prevent you from discovering midway through that you don't have an important ingredient or that a recipe requires several hours of marinating. And it's also a good idea to assemble all ingredients and utensils within easy reach before you begin a recipe.

Weighing and Measuring The success of any recipe depends on accurate weighing and measuring. The effectiveness of the Weight Watchers Program and the accuracy of the nutritional analysis depend on correct measuring as well. Use the following techniques:

▶ Weigh foods such as meat, poultry, and fish on a food scale.

▶ To measure liquids, use a standard glass or plastic measuring cup placed on a level surface. For amounts less than ¼ cup, use standard measuring spoons.

▶ To measure dry ingredients, use metal or plastic measuring cups that come in ¼-, ⅓-, ½-, and 1-cup sizes. Fill the appropriate cup, and level it with the flat edge of a knife or spatula. For amounts less than ¼ cup, use standard measuring spoons.

Spicy chicken breast is served with cool blue cheese dressing.
BUFFALO-STYLE GRILLED CHICKEN, PAGE 98

COOKING FOR
ONE ESSENTIALS

Dining alone needn't mean a meal of cheese and crackers, a frozen microwavable dinner, or even worse—fast-food takeout. Whether your table setting for one is because you live by yourself, because your partner often works late, or because the rest of the family isn't yet on board with healthy eating (though that may change when they see your scrumptious fare!), you'll find recipes here to quickly create fresh, satisfying meals just for you.

The majority of recipes in this cookbook serve one, but some give instructions for doubling the servings for those times when you're sharing a meal with another person. The last two chapters give instructions for storing and serving later for when you want to have ready-made meals or snacks to enjoy another day. Follow our tips for shopping, equipping the kitchen, and for what to do with the minimal, but inevitable, leftover ingredients to make cooking for yourself a pleasurable activity.

SMALL SCALE SHOPPING

When you're shopping for one, these tips will make it easy and economical in every aisle of the supermarket.

Meats, Poultry, and Seafood When you buy a large steak, such as a sirloin or a flank steak, cut it into single portions at home, and individually wrap each one. Refrigerate the servings if you plan to use them in two to three days, or for longer storage, place the meat in individual zip-close freezer bags and freeze up to three months. Ask for large packages of pork chops, chicken pieces, or lamb chops to be scaled down to one or two servings. Or, consider buying individually wrapped chicken breasts and boneless pork chops; they are more expensive but incredibly convenient. Shop for seafood at a supermarket or a specialty shop where you can buy as much or as little as you need.

Dairy and Eggs Depending on how much you use, buy fat-free or low-fat milk in pints or quarts; they may cost a little more than the larger sizes, but you'll have less waste. Buy cheeses in the deli section of the supermarket or at a store that sells them cut to order so you can buy just the amount you want. Cheese does not freeze well, so buy only what you'll use in about two weeks. Always keep eggs on hand; they are the ultimate food for cooking for one. (Enjoy them in Monterey Eggs, page 2, or Asparagus-Dill Frittata with Caviar, page 4.)

Produce Shop at a supermarket that carries loose produce where you can buy just one or two of items such as onions, bell peppers, zucchini, or bananas. Or choose the supermarket salad bar for items like sliced mushrooms, red onions, or shredded carrots when you need a small amount of an ingredient for a recipe.

Take advantage of small vegetables in the produce aisle. Use shallots instead of onions, Brussels sprouts instead of cabbage, and baby squash and potatoes instead of the standard versions. The price may be a little higher, but you'll have just what you need and no more.

Many fresh fruits are perfect for single people. Fruits such as apples, pears, oranges, peaches, plums, and nectarines are self-contained servings for one, either for a snack or for using in a recipe. They can be stored at room temperature for several days, and keeping them on the kitchen counter will remind you to enjoy a healthy *0 PointsPlus* value snack. For longer storage, keep fruits (except bananas) in the refrigerator.

Shop at farmers' markets whenever you can. They are more likely to sell produce by the pound or by the piece, so you can buy just what you need. And, the produce at farmers' markets is fresher and has a longer shelf life than that found in supermarkets. It was probably harvested the day before sale, and it hasn't had to travel a long distance.

Pantry Staples Seek out canned vegetables and beans that are available in smaller cans (usually 8 ½- or 11-ounces); they're perfect for one or two servings. Purchase single-serve containers of unsweetened applesauce and fruit packed in juice.

Keep quick-cooking grains such as bulgur, whole wheat couscous, and quinoa on hand so you can make a single serving as a side dish. Alternatively, cook a larger batch of a longer cooking grain, such as brown rice, wheat berries, or barley on the weekend, and serve it several times throughout the week.

Keep a stash of long-keeping condiments such as mustards, chutneys, soy sauce, hoisin sauce, and chili-garlic paste on hand to add flavor and interest to your meals.

Check the bulk bins at the supermarket for items you may not use that often or when you only want to buy a small amount. Look for whole grains, dried beans, lentils, nuts, dried fruit, and spices.

Buy plain unseasoned frozen vegetables in loose-packed bags. Unlike boxed frozen vegetables, you can take out only what you need. Avoid single-serve frozen vegetables; most of these contain high calorie sauces.

EQUIPMENT BASICS

You probably already have most of the equipment you need to cook on a small scale. Well-made cookware is expensive, so if you are missing a few of the basics, buy what you need over time. Don't forget to check thrift stores and yard sales for bargain-priced quality cookware. You can often find treasures for a fraction of their retail price.

Cookware Invest in a small 8- to 10-inch skillet, either standard or nonstick, or better yet—one of each. A 1½- or 2-quart saucepan is the perfect size for making a small batch of soup or cooking pasta for one. If you love the flavor of grilled food, but don't want to fire up the grill for one, invest in a cast-iron grill skillet or grill pan. Try out single-serve grilling with recipes such as Summer Steak Salad with Arugula and Dill, page 30, Paprika Pork with Grapefruit, page 90, or Buffalo-Style Grilled Chicken, page 98.

Bakeware Small casserole dishes or gratin dishes come in sizes ranging from 6- to 16-ounces and make it convenient to create recipes such as potpie, lasagna, fruit cobbler, or bread pudding for one. For many recipes, you can substitute ramekins that you may already have instead of using a special dish. If you frequently make desserts, invest in mini versions of bakeware such as Bundt pans, angel food cake–pans, and tart pans.

Appliances A toaster oven is the perfect countertop appliance for cooking for one. With the right small-sized bakeware, you can make almost anything in the toaster oven that you can in a large oven. And, you'll use less energy and generate less heat in the kitchen than you would with a regular oven. Though not absolutely necessary, a mini–food processor makes it easy to process a small amount of food. For mixing small quantities, an inexpensive handheld mixer will suffice.

Storage Containers The most convenient meals for one are dishes that you make in a large batch, store in single portions, and simply reheat for serving. Make sure you have lots of single-serve containers for storing leftovers. You can take the food to work to enjoy for lunch, or have it for dinner on nights when you don't want to cook. Check out our chapter, "Meals with Leftovers," page 162, for 25 recipes that make four servings with storing and reheating instructions.

LEFTOVER ODDS AND ENDS

Cooking for one often means you'll have an unused bit of an ingredient remaining after preparing a recipe. Try these ideas for using up what's leftover.

Cooked Meats, Poultry, Vegetables, and Grains Add to a salad, make soup using canned broth as the base, or mix with eggs and turn them into a frittata.

Canned Beans Give your meals a boost of protein and fiber by adding beans to soup or salad, stirring into salsa, or adding to taco or burrito fillings.

Tomato Products Transfer partial containers of canned diced tomatoes, stewed tomatoes, or tomato sauce to airtight containers and cover. Refrigerate up to 5 days or freeze up to 3 months. Add them to soups, stews, casseroles, or pasta dishes.

Pesto, Tomato Paste, Broths, and Coconut Milk Freeze these in ice cube trays and they'll be recipe-ready when you need just a tablespoon or two for a recipe.

Fresh Herbs Pop a sprig of mint, basil, tarragon, or rosemary into a glass of iced tea or sparkling water to add freshness and flavor. Or, to freeze fresh herbs, chop them, put them in ice cube trays, add water to cover, and freeze. Once frozen, store the cubes in a zip-close plastic bag. Use them in cooked dishes such as soups, stews, or pasta dishes. The small amount of water in the ice cube won't affect most recipes.

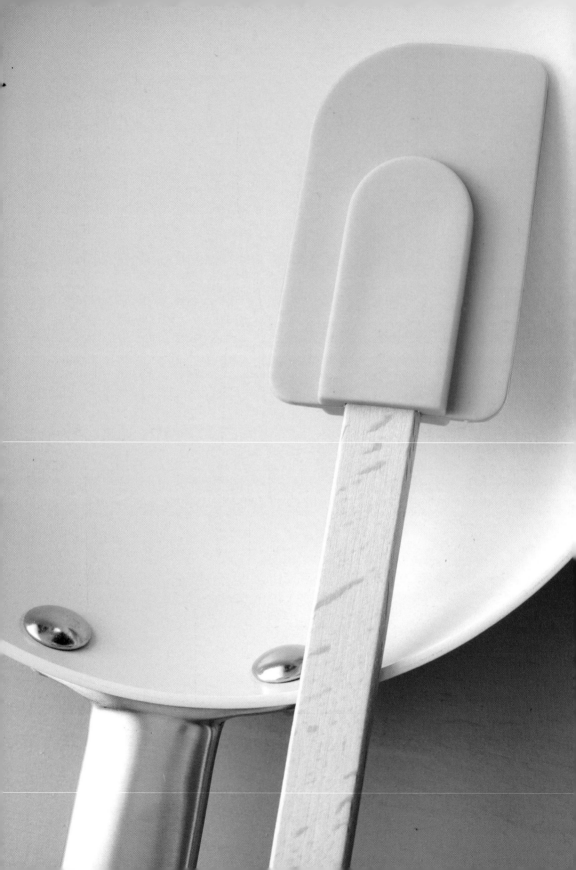

CHAPTER 1

EASY BREAKFASTS AND LUNCHES

Get out of your mealtime rut with creative options to fill you up.

MONTEREY EGGS

SERVES 1

▲ ½ **cup fat-free green salsa**

▲ 2 **large eggs**

2 **tablespoons shredded low-fat Monterey Jack cheese**

1 **tablespoon minced fresh cilantro**

1 Preheat oven to 400°F. Spray shallow 2-cup baking dish with nonstick spray.

2 Place salsa in prepared baking dish. Bake until salsa is hot, 10–15 minutes.

3 With back of spoon, make 2 wells in salsa and carefully break 1 egg into each well. Bake 5 minutes. Sprinkle eggs with Monterey Jack; bake until egg whites are opaque and yolks are almost set, about 5 minutes longer. Sprinkle with cilantro.

PER SERVING (1 dish): 220 Cal, 12 g Total Fat, 5 g Sat Fat, 0 g Trans Fat, 438 mg Chol, 705 mg Sod, 11 g Carb, 4 g Sugar, 0 g Fib, 16 g Prot, 240 mg Calc.

STAY ON TRACK

For an extra **2 PointsPlus** value, serve the eggs with a 7-inch whole wheat tortilla.

CRAB AND POTATO HASH WITH POACHED EGG

SERVES 1

▲ 1 **(5-ounce) Yukon Gold potato, scrubbed and diced**

▲ ⅓ **cup diced red bell pepper**

▲ ⅓ **cup diced celery**

▲ 3 **tablespoons minced red onion**

▲ 4 **ounces fresh or canned crabmeat, picked over**

▲ 2 **tablespoons reduced-sodium chicken broth**

½ **teaspoon salt-free Cajun seasoning**

1 **tablespoon minced fresh flat-leaf parsley**

▲ 1 **large egg**

1 Bring small saucepan of water to boil. Add potato; cook until almost tender, about 6 minutes. Drain.

2 Spray medium nonstick skillet with nonstick spray and set over medium heat. Add potato, bell pepper, celery, and onion. Cook, stirring often, until vegetables are tender, about 8 minutes.

3 Add crabmeat, broth, and Cajun seasoning; cook, stirring often, until crab is heated through, about 2 minutes. Remove from heat and stir in parsley.

4 Meanwhile, bring 2 inches of water just to boil in medium skillet. Reduce heat to very gentle simmer. Break egg into saucer, and then slip egg into skillet. Cook until white is set and yolk begins to thicken but not harden, 2–3 minutes.

5 Spoon hash onto plate. With slotted spoon, place egg on top of hash and serve at once.

PER SERVING (about 1 ½ cups hash and 1 egg): 370 Cal, 8 g Total Fat, 2 g Sat Fat, 0 g Trans Fat, 314 mg Chol, 625 mg Sod, 33 g Carb, 5 g Sugar, 4 g Fib, 38 g Prot, 213 mg Calc.

Fresh steamed asparagus makes an elegant accompaniment to this decadent brunch.

ASPARAGUS-DILL FRITTATA WITH CAVIAR

SERVES 1 UNDER 20 MINUTES

▲ 2 **large egg whites**

▲ 1 **large egg**

1 **teaspoon olive oil**

▲ 4 **asparagus spears, trimmed and cut into ½-inch pieces**

2 **tablespoons minced shallot**

2 **teaspoons minced fresh dill or ½ teaspoon dried**

⅛ **teaspoon salt**

⅛ **teaspoon black pepper**

▲ 1 **tablespoon fat-free sour cream**

1 **teaspoon black caviar**

1 Whisk together egg whites and egg in small bowl until blended. Set aside.

2 Heat oil in 8-inch nonstick skillet over medium heat. Add asparagus and shallot; cook, stirring often, until vegetables are softened, about 3 minutes. Stir in dill, salt, and pepper.

3 Add egg mixture and cover skillet. Reduce heat to low and cook, undisturbed, until bottom of frittata is firm, about 6 minutes. Transfer to plate; top with sour cream and caviar.

PER SERVING (1 frittata): 198 Cal, 10 g Total Fat, 2 g Sat Fat, 0 g Trans Fat, 248 mg Chol, 571 mg Sod, 11 g Carb, 3 g Sugar, 2 g Fib, 17 g Prot, 85 mg Calc.

FOR YOUR INFO

If you don't want to spring for the caviar to serve on top of the frittata, sprinkle it with a tablespoon of capers to add a pungent salty flavor for a fraction of the cost.

Try this super-quick frittata as a weekday treat.
ASPARAGUS-DILL FRITTATA WITH CAVIAR

BLACK BEAN HUEVOS RANCHEROS

SERVES 1

▲ ½ **cup canned fat-free refried black beans**

▲ ¼ **cup fat-free salsa**

▲ 1 **large egg**

1 **(6-inch) corn tortilla, warmed**

2 **teaspoons reduced-fat sour cream**

Chopped fresh cilantro

▲ **Thinly sliced scallions**

1 Spray small nonstick skillet with nonstick spray and set over medium heat. Add beans and 2 tablespoons salsa. Cook, stirring often, until heated through, about 3 minutes.

2 Meanwhile, spray another small nonstick skillet with nonstick spray and set over medium heat. Break egg into saucer, and then slip egg into skillet. Reduce heat and cook egg slowly until white is set and yolk begins to thicken, or turn egg to cook both sides.

3 Place tortilla on plate and spread with bean mixture. Top with egg, then with remaining 2 tablespoons salsa, sour cream, cilantro, and scallions. Serve at once.

PER SERVING (1 heuvo ranchero): 301 Cal, 7 g Total Fat, 2 g Sat Fat, 0 g Trans Fat, 187 mg Chol, 834 mg Sod, 43 g Carb, 4 g Sugar, 9 g Fib, 17 g Prot, 103 mg Calc.

APPLE AND HONEY IRISH OATMEAL

SERVES 1

½ cup water

½ cup apple cider
or juice

▲ ¼ cup steel-cut oats

Pinch salt

1 teaspoon honey

▲ ½ small apple, chopped

1 Combine water, apple cider, oats, and salt in medium microwavable bowl. Cover with wax paper and microwave on High 3 minutes. Let stand at room temperature 30 minutes. Cover and refrigerate overnight.

2 Add honey to oat mixture; stir to mix well. Cover and microwave on High 3 minutes. Stir; then cover and let stand 10 minutes. Top with apple and serve at once.

PER SERVING (¾ cup oatmeal with ½ cup apple):
270 Cal, 3 g Total Fat, 1 g Sat Fat, 0 g Trans Fat, 0 mg Chol, 162 mg Sod, 58 g Carb, 27 g Sugar, 6 g Fib, 5 g Prot, 8 mg Calc.

Be sure to use real maple syrup for authentic flavor.
BANANA-STUFFED CINNAMON-RAISIN FRENCH TOAST

BANANA-STUFFED CINNAMON-RAISIN FRENCH TOAST

SERVES 1

2 tablespoons fat-free cream cheese, at room temperature

2 (⅜-inch-thick) slices cinnamon-raisin bread

▲ ¼ cup thinly sliced banana

▲ ¼ cup fat-free egg substitute

▲ ½ tablespoon fat-free milk

⅛ teaspoon vanilla extract

1 teaspoon pure maple syrup

1 Spread 1 tablespoon cream cheese on one side of each slice of bread. Top one slice with banana; top with remaining slice of bread.

2 Whisk together egg substitute, milk, and vanilla in small shallow bowl. Briefly dip sandwich into egg mixture.

3 Spray medium nonstick skillet with nonstick spray and set over medium heat. Place sandwich in skillet. Cook until golden brown, 3–4 minutes on each side. Place on plate; top with maple syrup and serve at once.

PER SERVING (1 stuffed French toast): 296 Cal, 5 g Total Fat, 0 g Sat Fat, 0 g Trans Fat, 5 mg Chol, 553 mg Sod, 46 g Carb, 24 g Sugar, 3 g Fib, 17 g Prot, 170 mg Calc.

STAY ON TRACK Top the French toast with fresh strawberries, raspberries, or blueberries.

BEEF AND MUSHROOM QUESADILLA WITH RED PEPPER SALSA

SERVES 1   UNDER 20 MINUTES

▲ 1   **plum tomato, diced**

▲ ¼   **cup diced roasted red bell pepper (not oil-packed)**

1   **tablespoon chopped fresh parsley**

½   **teaspoon red-wine vinegar**

   Pinch cayenne

½   **teaspoon olive oil**

▲ 2   **cups sliced white mushrooms**

▲ ¼   **cup chopped onion**

1   **(8-inch) fat-free whole wheat tortilla**

▲ 1   **ounce thinly sliced cooked lean sirloin, trimmed**

1   **ounce reduced-fat provolone cheese**

1 To make salsa, stir together tomato, bell pepper, parsley, vinegar, and cayenne in small bowl. Set aside.

2 Heat oil in medium nonstick skillet over medium heat. Add mushrooms and onion; cook, stirring occasionally, until lightly browned and tender, about 6 minutes. Transfer to plate.

3 Wipe out skillet. Spoon mushroom mixture over half of tortilla; top with sirloin and provolone. Fold other half of tortilla over filling and press lightly. Place quesadilla in skillet and set over medium heat. Cook, turning once, until cheese is melted and tortilla is lightly browned, about 2 minutes. Serve with salsa.

PER SERVING (1 quesadilla and ¾ cup salsa): 327 Cal, 9 g Total Fat, 4 g Sat Fat, 0 g Trans Fat, 26 mg Chol, 972 mg Sod, 41 g Carb, 8 g Sugar, 8 g Fib, 21 g Prot, 288 mg Calc.

8 PointsPlus® value

QUICK MOO SHU PORK WRAP

SERVES 1   UNDER 20 MINUTES

½   teaspoon canola oil

▲ 1   (¼-pound) lean boneless pork loin chop, trimmed and cut into strips

2   teaspoons hoisin sauce

▲ 2   cups coleslaw mix

1   (8-inch) fat-free whole wheat tortilla, warmed

▲ 1   scallion, sliced

1 Heat oil in medium nonstick skillet over medium heat. Add pork and cook, stirring often, until just cooked through, about 2 minutes. Transfer to plate. Toss with 1 teaspoon hoisin sauce.

2 Add coleslaw mix to skillet; cook, stirring often, until crisp-tender, about 2 minutes.

3 Spread tortilla with remaining 1 teaspoon hoisin sauce. Top with coleslaw, pork, and scallion. Roll up tortilla to enclose filling.

PER SERVING (1 wrap): 326 Cal, 9 g Total Fat, 2 g Sat Fat, 0 g Trans Fat, 67 mg Chol, 529 mg Sod, 35 g Carb, 3 g Sugar, 8 g Fib, 28 g Prot, 98 mg Calc.

8 PointsPlus© value

STAY ON TRACK

Mushrooms are a delicious addition to this wrap: Add ½ cup sliced shitake mushroom caps when you add the coleslaw mix in step 2.

BUFFALO–BLUE CHEESE CHICKEN SLIDERS

SERVES 1   UNDER 20 MINUTES

▲ 1   **tablespoon plain fat-free yogurt**

1   **tablespoon fat-free mayonnaise**

1   **teaspoon apple cider vinegar**

▲ ½   **cup shredded romaine lettuce**

▲ ¼   **cup thinly sliced celery**

1   **tablespoon crumbled reduced-fat blue cheese**

▲ 1   **tablespoon chopped red onion**

½   **teaspoon canola oil**

▲ 1   **(3-ounce) thin-sliced chicken breast cutlet**

2   **teaspoons hot pepper sauce**

2   **small whole wheat dinner rolls, split and toasted**

1 Combine yogurt, mayonnaise, and vinegar in small bowl. Add lettuce, celery, blue cheese, and onion; toss to coat. Set aside.

2 Heat oil in medium nonstick skillet over medium heat. Add chicken and cook, turning once, until browned and cooked through, 6 minutes. Transfer to cutting board and cut into thin strips; then transfer to second small bowl. Drizzle chicken with hot pepper sauce and toss to coat. Fill rolls with chicken and lettuce mixture.

PER SERVING (2 sliders): 338 Cal, 11 g Total Fat, 3 g Sat Fat, 0 g Trans Fat, 59 mg Chol, 847 mg Sod, 36g Carb, 9 g Sugar, 6 g Fib, 28 g Prot, 220 mg Calc.

Small whole wheat dinner rolls make perfect slider buns.
BUFFALO–BLUE CHEESE CHICKEN SLIDERS

VIETNAMESE CHICKEN SANDWICH WITH QUICK PICKLED VEGETABLES

SERVES 1 UNDER 20 MINUTES

- ▲ 1 **small carrot, shredded**
- ▲ 2 **tablespoons thinly sliced red onion**
- 2 **tablespoons chopped fresh cilantro**
- 1 **tablespoon rice vinegar**
- ½ **teaspoon chili-garlic paste**
- ▲ 1 **(3-ounce) thin-sliced chicken breast cutlet**
- 1 **tablespoon lime juice**
- 1 **small garlic clove, minced**
- 1 **(5-inch) piece whole-grain baguette, cut in half lengthwise**

1 To make pickled vegetables, combine carrot, onion, cilantro, vinegar, and chili paste in small bowl; toss to coat. Let stand at room temperature.

2 Place chicken in small shallow dish. Add lime juice and garlic, and turn chicken to coat.

3 Spray ridged cast-iron grill pan with nonstick spray and set over medium-high heat. Add chicken and cook, turning once, until browned and cooked through, about 4 minutes.

4 Place chicken on bottom half of baguette; top evenly with pickled vegetables. Cover with top of baguette.

PER SERVING (1 sandwich): 276 Cal, 4 g Total Fat, 1 g Sat Fat, 0 g Trans Fat, 47 mg Chol, 445 mg Sod, 38 g Carb, 6 g Sugar, 5 g Fib, 24 g Prot, 36 mg Calc.

FOR YOUR INFO

Chili-garlic paste is a spicy condiment used in Malaysian and Vietnamese cuisine. It's a mixture of chiles, vinegar, and salt. Look for it in the Asian section of most supermarkets.

CHIPOTLE CHICKEN TOSTADA

SERVES 1   UNDER 20 MINUTES

▲ 1   **(3-ounce) thin-sliced chicken breast cutlet**

   1   **small garlic clove, minced**

   ⅛   **teaspoon salt**

   ⅛   **teaspoon black pepper**

   ½   **teaspoon olive oil**

▲ 1   **plum tomato, chopped**

▲ 1   **tablespoon minced red onion**

   1   **tablespoon chopped fresh parsley**

   1   **tablespoon chopped fresh cilantro**

   ¼   **teaspoon minced chipotles en adobo**

   1   **(6-inch) corn tostada shell**

▲ ½   **cup thinly sliced romaine**

   Lime wedge

1 Sprinkle chicken with garlic, salt, and pepper. Heat oil in medium nonstick skillet over medium heat. Add chicken and cook, turning once, until browned and cooked through, 6 minutes. Transfer to cutting board and cut into thin strips.

2 Meanwhile, stir together tomato, onion, parsley, cilantro, and chipotles in small bowl. Place tostada shell on plate. Place chicken on tostada, top with romaine and tomato mixture. Serve with lime wedge.

PER SERVING (1 tostada): 240 Cal, 9 g Total Fat, 3 g Sat Fat, 0 g Trans Fat, 53 mg Chol, 468 mg Sod, 18 g Carb, 3 g Sugar, 3 g Fib, 22 g Prot, 54 mg Calc.

SOUTHWESTERN TURKEY AND AVOCADO SANDWICH

SERVES 1   UNDER 20 MINUTES

1	**tablespoon chopped fresh cilantro**
2	**teaspoons reduced-fat mayonnaise**
½	**teaspoon minced chipotles en adobo**
½	**teaspoon lime juice**
1	**(3-ounce) whole-grain bagel, split and toasted**
▲ 2	**slices tomato**
▲ 2	**ounces thinly sliced skinless smoked turkey breast**
⅛	**Hass avocado, peeled and sliced**

1 Stir together cilantro, mayonnaise, chipotles, and lime juice in small bowl. Spread on bottom half of bagel.

2 Top with tomato, turkey, and avocado. Cover with top half of bagel.

PER SERVING (1 sandwich): 296 Cal, 8 g Total Fat, 1 g Sat Fat, 0 g Trans Fat, 26 mg Chol, 851 mg Sod, 46 g Carb, 7 g Sugar, 8 g Fib, 18 g Prot, 208 mg Calc.

 FOR YOUR INFO To keep the leftover avocado fresh, keep the peel on and drizzle the cut surface with lime juice. Wrap the avocado in plastic wrap and refrigerate.

SEASIDE SHRIMP ROLL WITH TARRAGON

SERVES 1   UNDER 20 MINUTES

- ▲ 1 **tablespoon plain fat-free yogurt**
- 2 **teaspoons reduced-fat mayonnaise**
- 2 **teaspoons lemon juice**
- **Pinch black pepper**
- ▲ 1½ **tablespoons sliced scallion**
- 1½ **tablespoons chopped fresh tarragon**
- ▲ ¼ **pound cooked peeled and deveined medium shrimp, each cut in half**
- ▲ ¼ **cup diced English (seedless) cucumber**
- ▲ ½ **cup shredded romaine lettuce**
- ▲ 1 **reduced-calorie whole wheat hot dog bun, split and toasted**

1 Stir together yogurt, mayonnaise, lemon juice, and pepper in medium bowl; stir in scallion and tarragon.

2 Add shrimp and cucumber to bowl, and toss to coat. Place lettuce in bun; fill with shrimp mixture.

PER SERVING (1 sandwich): 268 Cal, 5 g Total Fat, 1 g Sat Fat, 0 g Trans Fat, 221 mg Chol, 562 mg Sod, 28 g Carb, 7 g Sugar, 4 g Fib, 29 g Prot, 152 mg Calc.

7 PointsPlus® value

GARLICKY BROCCOLI RABE AND FONTINA SANDWICH

SERVES 1   UNDER 20 MINUTES

▲ **3 cups trimmed and chopped broccoli rabe**

¼ cup water

½ teaspoon olive oil

1 garlic clove, sliced

▲ **¼ cup thinly sliced roasted red bell peppers (not oil-packed)**

⅛ teaspoon salt

Pinch red pepper flakes

2 tablespoons shredded fontina cheese

1 slice whole-grain country bread, toasted

1 Combine broccoli rabe and water in medium saucepan; bring to boil over high heat. Reduce heat and cover. Simmer until tender, about 3 minutes. Drain.

2 Heat oil in medium nonstick skillet over medium heat. Add garlic and cook, stirring constantly, until fragrant, 1 minute. Add broccoli rabe, bell peppers, salt, and pepper flakes. Cook, stirring often, until heated through, 2 minutes.

3 Sprinkle broccoli rabe mixture with fontina. Cover and cook until cheese is melted, 30 seconds. Top bread with broccoli rabe mixture.

PER SERVING (1 open-face sandwich): 327 Cal, 9 g Total Fat, 4 g Sat Fat, 0 g Trans Fat, 19 mg Chol, 935 mg Sod, 44 g Carb, 11 g Sugar, 3 g Fib, 19 g Prot, 568 mg Calc.

STAY ON TRACK Make a tomato salad by tossing together 1 tomato, cut into wedges; 1 teaspoon chopped fresh oregano; 1 teaspoon balsamic vinegar; and salt and black pepper to taste.

*Eat your greens in a
great-tasting sandwich.*
**GARLICKY BROCCOLI RABE
AND FONTINA SANDWICH**

GRILLED MOZZARELLA, TOMATO, AND TAPENADE SANDWICH

SERVES 1   UNDER 20 MINUTES

2   **thin slices whole-grain Italian bread**

1   **teaspoon olive tapenade**

▲ 3   **slices tomato**

1   **(1-ounce) slice reduced-fat mozzarella**

4   **large fresh basil leaves**

½   **teaspoon olive oil**

1 Spread one side of each bread slice with tapenade. Layer tomato, mozzarella, and basil on 1 slice; top with remaining slice.

2 Heat oil in medium nonstick skillet over medium heat. Add sandwich and cook until underside is lightly browned and crisp, about 2 minutes. With spatula, flip sandwich, and cook until bottom is browned, about 2 minutes. Serve at once.

PER SERVING (1 sandwich): 214 Cal, 9 g Total Fat, 3 g Sat Fat, 0 g Trans Fat, 15 mg Chol, 503 mg Sod, 21 g Carb, 3 g Sugar, 3 g Fib, 9 g Prot, 438 mg Calc.

GOAT CHEESE QUESADILLA WITH CORN AND POBLANO

SERVES 1   UNDER 20 MINUTES

½   **teaspoon canola oil**

 1   **small poblano pepper, diced**

▲ ½   **cup fresh corn kernels**

1   **(8-inch) fat-free whole wheat tortilla**

¼   **cup reduced-fat soft goat cheese, at room temperature**

1   **tablespoon chopped fresh cilantro**

▲ 2   **tablespoons fat-free salsa**

1 Heat oil in medium nonstick skillet over medium heat. Add poblano and corn; cook, stirring often, until vegetables are tender, about 5 minutes. Transfer to plate.

2 Wipe out skillet. Spoon poblano mixture over half of tortilla; top with goat cheese and cilantro. Fold other half of tortilla over filling and press lightly.

3 Place quesadilla in skillet and set over medium heat. Cook, turning once, until cheese is melted and tortilla is lightly browned, about 2 minutes. Serve with salsa.

PER SERVING (1 quesadilla): 291 Cal, 8 g Total Fat, 2 g Sat Fat, 0 g Trans Fat, 5 mg Chol, 523 mg Sod, 48 g Carb, 5 g Sugar, 9 g Fib, 13 g Prot, 52 mg Calc.

FOR YOUR INFO Not a fan of goat cheese? Substitute ¼ cup shredded reduced-fat Monterey Jack or Cheddar cheese for the goat cheese.

CHICKEN SOUP WITH QUINOA, CORN, AND ZUCCHINI

SERVES 1   UNDER 20 MINUTES

- ½ **teaspoon olive oil**
- ▲ ½ **cup fresh or thawed frozen corn kernels**
- ▲ ¼ **cup diced onion**
- 1 **small garlic clove, minced**
- ½ **teaspoon ground cumin**
- ▲ 1 **cup reduced-sodium chicken broth**
- ¼ **cup water**
- ▲ 3 **tablespoons quinoa, rinsed**
- ▲ 1 **small zucchini, diced (about 2 cups)**
- ▲ 1 **(3-ounce) thin-sliced chicken breast cutlet, diced**
- ▲ 1 **plum tomato, diced**
- 2 **tablespoons chopped fresh cilantro**
- **Lime wedge**

1 Heat oil in small saucepan over medium heat. Add corn and onion; cook, stirring frequently, until softened, about 5 minutes. Add garlic and cumin. Cook, stirring constantly until fragrant, 1 minute.

2 Add broth and water and bring to boil. Stir in quinoa. Reduce heat and simmer 5 minutes. Stir in zucchini and chicken. Simmer until quinoa and zucchini are tender and chicken is cooked through, about 5 minutes longer.

3 Remove from heat and stir in tomato and cilantro. Serve with lime wedge.

PER SERVING (2 cups): 388 Cal, 9 g Total Fat, 2 g Sat Fat, 0 g Trans Fat, 47 mg Chol, 148 mg Sod, 49 g Carb, 8 g Sugar, 7 g Fib, 32 g Prot, 83 mg Calc.

MOROCCAN CHICKEN, VEGETABLE, AND COUSCOUS SOUP

SERVES 1 UNDER 20 MINUTES

½ teaspoon olive oil

▲ 1 cup diced butternut squash

▲ ½ cup diced onion

½ teaspoon minced garlic

½ teaspoon ground cumin

⅛ teaspoon cinnamon

▲ 1¼ cups reduced-sodium chicken broth

▲ ½ cup canned diced tomatoes

▲ 1 (¼-pound) skinless boneless chicken breast, diced

▲ 2 tablespoons whole wheat couscous

2 teaspoons lemon juice

1 Heat oil in small saucepan over medium-high heat. Add squash and onion; cook, stirring frequently, until lightly browned, about 5 minutes. Add garlic, cumin, and cinnamon. Cook, stirring constantly, until fragrant, about 1 minute.

2 Add broth and tomatoes and bring to boil. Add chicken. Reduce heat and cover. Simmer, stirring occasionally, until chicken is cooked through and squash is tender, about 5 minutes.

3 Remove from heat; stir in couscous. Cover and let stand until couscous is tender, about 5 minutes. Stir in lemon juice.

PER SERVING (1 ¾ cups): 382 Cal, 8 g Total Fat, 2 g Sat Fat, 0 g Trans Fat, 63 mg Chol, 445 mg Sod, 47 g Carb, 11 g Sugar, 7 g Fib, 34 g Prot, 146 mg Calc.

SPICY CHICKPEA AND BROCCOLI SOUP

SERVES 1   UNDER 20 MINUTES

1   **teaspoon olive oil**

1   **small garlic clove, minced**

▲ 1   **cup reduced-sodium chicken broth**

▲ ½   **cup canned diced tomatoes**

⅛   **teaspoon red pepper flakes**

▲ 1   **cup small broccoli florets**

▲ ½   **cup canned chickpeas, rinsed and drained**

2   **teaspoons grated Parmesan cheese**

1   Heat oil in small saucepan over medium heat. Add garlic and cook, stirring constantly, until fragrant, about 1 minute.

2   Add broth, tomatoes, and pepper flakes; bring to boil. Add broccoli and chickpeas; reduce heat and cover. Simmer, stirring occasionally, until broccoli is tender, about 5 minutes.

3   Transfer to bowl; sprinkle with Parmesan.

PER SERVING (1 ¾ cups): 248 Cal, 9 g Total Fat, 2 g Sat Fat, 0 g Trans Fat, 3 mg Chol, 713 mg Sod, 31 g Carb, 6 g Sugar, 7 g Fib, 14 g Prot, 126 mg Calc.

FOR YOUR INFO For a delicious variation on this soup, use cauliflower instead of broccoli and cannellini beans instead of chickpeas.

BUTTERNUT-BULGUR CHILI

SERVES 1   UNDER 20 MINUTES

1   **teaspoon olive oil**

▲ **½**   **cup chopped yellow bell pepper**

▲ **⅓**   **cup chopped onion**

1   **small garlic clove, minced**

1¼   **teaspoons chili powder**

½   **teaspoon smoked paprika**

▲ **1**   **cup diced butternut squash**

¾   **cup water**

▲ **¾**   **cup canned crushed tomatoes**

▲ **⅓**   **cup bulgur**

2   **tablespoons chopped fresh cilantro**

1   Heat oil in small saucepan over medium heat. Add bell pepper and onion; cook, stirring occasionally, until softened, about 5 minutes.

2   Add garlic, chili powder, and smoked paprika. Cook, stirring constantly, until fragrant, about 1 minute.

3   Add squash, water, tomatoes, and bulgur; bring to boil. Reduce heat and cover. Simmer, stirring occasionally, until vegetables and bulgur are tender, about 10 minutes. Remove from heat; stir in cilantro.

PER SERVING (about 2 cups): 378 Cal, 7 g Total Fat, 1 g Sat Fat, 0 g Trans Fat, 0 mg Chol, 312 mg Sod, 77 g Carb, 8 g Sugar, 19 g Fib, 12 g Prot, 190 mg Calc.

FOR YOUR INFO

Smoked paprika is made by smoking dried red bell peppers over a wood fire. It adds flame-kissed flavor to any dish without having to light up the grill.

A sprinkle of cracked black pepper lends a spicy bite.
TOMATO-FENNEL SOUP WITH YOGURT

TOMATO-FENNEL SOUP WITH YOGURT

SERVES 1   UNDER 20 MINUTES

1   teaspoon olive oil

▲ ½   fennel bulb, diced (1 ½ cups)

▲ ⅓   cup chopped onion

2   garlic cloves, minced

▲ 1   cup canned diced tomatoes

▲ ½   cup reduced-sodium chicken broth

1   tablespoon chopped fennel fronds

▲ 1   tablespoon plain fat-free Greek yogurt

1   Heat oil in small saucepan over medium heat. Add fennel, onion, and garlic. Cook, stirring occasionally, until softened, about 5 minutes.

2   Add tomatoes and broth; bring to boil. Reduce heat and cover. Simmer until vegetables are very tender, about 8 minutes. Let cool 5 minutes.

3   Puree soup in blender or food processor. Transfer to bowl. Sprinkle with fennel fronds and top with yogurt.

PER SERVING (1 ¾ cups soup and 1 tablespoon yogurt): 181 Cal, 6 g Total Fat, 1 g Sat Fat, 0 g Trans Fat, 0 mg Chol, 648 mg Sod, 27 g Carb, 12 g Sugar, 5 g Fib, 7 g Prot, 105 mg Calc.

FOR YOUR INFO   Always save the bright green fronds from the top of a fennel bulb. Chop them and use them as you would any fresh herb to add anise flavor to soups, salads, or side dishes.

PARSNIP-APPLE SOUP WITH BLUE CHEESE

SERVES 1

▲ 1 **large parsnip (6 ounces), peeled and cut into ¾-inch chunks (1 ⅓ cups)**

▲ 1 **Granny Smith apple, peeled, cored, and cut into large chunks**

▲ 1 **small onion, cut into large chunks**

 1 **teaspoon canola oil**

 ⅛ **teaspoon salt**

 Pinch black pepper

▲ 1 **cup reduced-sodium vegetable broth**

 ¼ **cup water**

 ¼ **teaspoon dried thyme**

 1 **tablespoon crumbled blue cheese**

1 Preheat oven to 425°F. Spray small rimmed baking sheet with nonstick spray.

2 Place parsnip, apple, and onion on prepared baking sheet. Drizzle with oil and sprinkle with salt and pepper; toss to coat. Roast, stirring occasionally, until vegetables are tender, about 35 minutes.

3 Place roasted vegetables in blender or food processor. Add broth and puree. Transfer mixture to small saucepan. Add water and thyme. Bring to simmer over medium heat, stirring occasionally. Transfer soup to bowl; sprinkle with blue cheese.

PER SERVING (1 ½ cups soup and 1 tablespoon blue cheese): 332 Cal, 8 g Total Fat, 2 g Sat Fat, 0 g Trans Fat, 6 mg Chol, 570 mg Sod, 65 g Carb, 35 g Sugar, 11 g Fib, 5 g Prot, 158 mg Calc.

9 PointsPlus© value

PROSCIUTTO AND MOZZARELLA PANZANELLA

SERVES 1

▲ 1 **tomato, cut into 1-inch chunks**

▲ 2 **tablespoons diced red onion**

1 **teaspoon red-wine vinegar**

½ **teaspoon olive oil**

⅛ **teaspoon black pepper**

1 **thin slice whole-grain Italian bread**

1 **garlic clove, peeled and cut in half**

1 **ounce fresh mozzarella, cut into ½-inch pieces**

1 **ounce prosciutto, cut into thin strips**

4 **fresh basil leaves, thinly sliced**

1 Stir together tomato, onion, vinegar, oil, and pepper in medium bowl. Let stand, stirring occasionally, until tomatoes begin to release their juices, about 15 minutes.

2 Toast bread and rub with cut garlic clove; cut bread into ½-inch pieces. Discard garlic clove. Add bread, mozzarella, prosciutto, and basil to tomato mixture; toss to combine. Serve at once.

PER SERVING (3 cups): 246 Cal, 12 g Total Fat, 5 g Sat Fat, 0 g Trans Fat, 38 mg Chol, 864 mg Sod, 19 g Carb, 5 g Sugar, 6 g Fib, 16 g Prot, 113 mg Calc.

FOR YOUR INFO

Panzanella salad is perfect for using up day old bread that you have on hand. The juices from the tomato soak into the bread to flavor and soften it.

SUMMER STEAK SALAD
WITH ARUGULA AND DILL

SERVES 1   UNDER 20 MINUTES

▲ 1   **(¼-pound) piece lean boneless sirloin steak, trimmed**

¼   **teaspoon salt**

2   **pinches black pepper**

1   **tablespoon white-wine vinegar**

2   **teaspoons water**

1   **teaspoon olive oil**

¼   **teaspoon Dijon mustard**

1   **teaspoon minced shallot**

▲ ½   **cup halved cherry tomatoes**

▲ ½   **cup sliced English (seedless) cucumber**

▲ 1   **radish, thinly sliced**

2   **tablespoons chopped fresh dill**

▲ 2   **cups lightly packed baby arugula**

1 Sprinkle steak with ⅛ teaspoon salt and 1 pinch pepper. Spray ridged cast-iron grill pan with nonstick spray and set over medium-high heat. Add steak and cook, turning once, until instant-read thermometer inserted into side of steak registers 145°F for medium, about 6 minutes. Transfer steak to cutting board and let stand 3 minutes. Cut into thin slices.

2 Meanwhile, to make dressing, stir together vinegar, water, oil, mustard, shallot, remaining ⅛ teaspoon salt, and remaining 1 pinch of pepper in medium bowl.

3 Add tomatoes, cucumber, radish, and dill to bowl; toss to combine.

4 Arrange arugula on plate. Using slotted spoon, place tomato mixture on arugula. Top with sliced steak. Drizzle steak with remaining dressing in bowl.

PER SERVING (1 plate): 232 Cal, 10 g Total Fat, 3 g Sat Fat, 0 g Trans Fat, 49 mg Chol, 685 mg Sod, 7 g Carb, 4 g Sugar, 2 g Fib, 28 g Prot, 103 mg Calc.

6
PointsPlus
value

DOUBLE IT

To make the salad for two, use 1 (½-pound) piece lean boneless sirloin steak, trimmed, and double all the remaining ingredients. Increase the cooking time for the steak to 8 minutes.

Baby salad greens are a mild-flavored substitute for arugula.
SUMMER STEAK SALAD WITH ARUGULA AND DILL

SALADE AUX LARDONS

SERVES 1   UNDER 20 MINUTES

1   **teaspoon olive oil**

2   **(1-ounce) slices Canadian bacon, cut into thin strips**

2   **tablespoons minced shallot**

1   **tablespoon white-wine vinegar**

½   **teaspoon Dijon mustard**

½   **teaspoon Worcestershire sauce**

½   **teaspoon minced fresh thyme**

▲ 2   **cups torn frisée**

▲ 1   **large egg**

1 Heat oil in small nonstick skillet over medium heat. Add Canadian bacon and cook until crisp, stirring often, about 4 minutes. With slotted spoon, transfer bacon to large bowl.

2 Add shallot to same skillet and cook, stirring constantly, until softened, 2 minutes. Add vinegar, mustard, Worcestershire sauce, and thyme; bring to boil, stirring constantly. Add shallot mixture to bowl with Canadian bacon. Add frisée to bowl; toss to coat. Transfer salad to plate.

3 Meanwhile, bring 2 inches of water just to boil in medium skillet. Reduce heat to very gentle simmer. Break egg into saucer, and then slip egg into skillet. Cook until white is set and yolk begins to thicken but not harden, 2–3 minutes. With slotted spoon, place egg on top of salad and serve at once.

PER SERVING (1 salad): 207 Cal, 12 g Total Fat, 3 g Sat Fat, 0 g Trans Fat, 236 mg Chol, 736 mg Sod, 8 g Carb, 2 g Sugar, 3 g Fib, 16 g Prot, 91 mg Calc.

FOR YOUR INFO

Salade aux Lardons is a classic French salad typically made with strips of thick-cut bacon. You'll find this healthier version made with Canadian bacon to be equally delicious.

MANGO-MINT CHICKEN AND BLACK BEAN SALAD

SERVES 1 UNDER 20 MINUTES

¼ **teaspoon grated orange zest**

2 **tablespoons orange juice**

2 **teaspoons apple cider vinegar**

1 **teaspoon olive oil**

¼ **teaspoon ground cumin**

⅛ **teaspoon salt**

▲ 1 **orange, peeled and cut into segments**

▲ ½ **cup shredded cooked skinless chicken breast**

▲ ½ **cup canned black beans, rinsed and drained**

▲ ⅓ **cup diced mango**

▲ ¼ **cup diced jicama**

▲ 1 **tablespoon diced red onion**

▲ 1 **teaspoon minced jalapeño pepper**

2 **tablespoons chopped fresh mint**

1 Stir together orange zest and juice, vinegar, oil, cumin, and salt in medium bowl.

2 Add orange segments, chicken, beans, mango, jicama, onion, jalapeño, and mint; toss to combine.

PER SERVING (2 cups): 392 Cal, 8 g Total Fat, 1 g Sat Fat, 0 g Trans Fat, 60 mg Chol, 748 mg Sod, 51 g Carb, 21 g Sugar, 11 g Fib, 30 g Prot, 131 mg Calc.

FOR YOUR INFO

To use leftover jicama, cut it into sticks and serve it with salsa for a snack or with hummus for a light lunch.

SUSHI-STYLE SHRIMP SALAD

SERVES 1

¼ cup water

▲ ¼ cup quick-cooking brown rice

1½ tablespoons rice vinegar

½ teaspoon canola oil

1 teaspoon minced pickled ginger

½ teaspoon wasabi paste

¼ teaspoon sugar

¼ teaspoon reduced-sodium soy sauce

▲ ¼ pound cooked peeled and deveined medium shrimp

▲ ¼ cup diced English (seedless) cucumber

▲ ¼ cup shredded carrot

2 tablespoons chopped avocado

▲ 1 tablespoon sliced scallion

▲ 4 leaves Bibb or green leaf lettuce

¼ teaspoon toasted sesame seeds

1 Bring water to boil in small saucepan. Add rice; cover and cook over medium-low heat until tender, about 5 minutes. Transfer to small bowl to cool.

2 Whisk together vinegar, oil, ginger, wasabi paste, sugar, and soy sauce in medium bowl. Add rice, shrimp, cucumber, carrot, avocado, and scallion; toss to combine.

3 Place lettuce on plate. Top with shrimp salad and sprinkle with sesame seeds.

PER SERVING (1 plate): 292 Cal, 7 g Total Fat, 1 g Sat Fat, 0 g Trans Fat, 221 mg Chol, 437 mg Sod, 29 g Carb, 4 g Sugar, 5 g Fib, 28 g Prot, 115 mg Calc.

7 PointsPlus® value

FOR YOUR INFO

You can use leftover cooked brown rice for this recipe—you'll need ⅓ cup.

LOBSTER, ARUGULA, AND APPLE SALAD

SERVES 1   UNDER 20 MINUTES

  1   **(6-ounce) shell-on lobster tail**

1½   **teaspoons sherry vinegar**

1   **teaspoon extra-virgin olive oil**

½   **teaspoon Dijon mustard**

⅛   **teaspoon salt**

⅛   **teaspoon black pepper**

  1   **cup baby arugula**

  2   **large radishes, cut into matchstick strips**

  ½   **Granny Smith apple, cored and cut into matchstick strips**

1 Bring medium saucepan of water to boil over medium-high heat. Add lobster tail and cook until shell turns bright red, 6–8 minutes. Using tongs, transfer lobster tail to colander and rinse under cold running water until cool enough to handle. Using kitchen scissors, cut shell in half lengthwise and remove meat. Thinly slice lobster tail.

2 Whisk together vinegar, oil, mustard, salt, and pepper in medium bowl. Add arugula, radishes, and apple; toss to coat. Place salad on plate; top with sliced lobster.

PER SERVING (1 salad): 253 Cal, 7 g Total Fat, 1 g Sat Fat, 0 g Trans Fat, 162 mg Chol, 868 mg Sod, 15 g Carb, 10 g Sugar, 3 g Fib, 33 g Prot, 125 mg Calc.

FOR YOUR INFO If you don't want to splurge on lobster, you can skip step 1 and use 3 ounces cooked peeled and deveined shrimp.

CHICKPEA AND COUSCOUS SALAD WITH PISTACHIOS

SERVES 1   UNDER 20 MINUTES

½ **cup water**

▲ ¼ **cup whole wheat couscous**

3 **tablespoons orange juice**

2 **teaspoons apple cider vinegar**

1 **teaspoon olive oil**

¼ **teaspoon ground cumin**

⅛ **teaspoon salt**

Pinch cinnamon

Pinch cayenne

▲ ⅓ **cup canned chickpeas, rinsed and drained**

2 **tablespoons chopped fresh mint**

▲ 1 **scallion, thinly sliced**

2 **dried apricots, diced**

▲ 1 **cup lightly packed baby spinach**

1 **tablespoon unsalted chopped pistachios**

1 Bring water to boil in small saucepan; remove from heat and stir in couscous. Cover and let stand 5 minutes. Fluff with fork.

2 Meanwhile, whisk together orange juice, vinegar, oil, cumin, salt, cinnamon, and cayenne in medium bowl. Add couscous, chickpeas, mint, scallion, and apricots; toss to combine.

3 Place spinach on plate. Top with couscous mixture and sprinkle with pistachios.

PER SERVING (1 plate): 318 Cal, 10 g Total Fat, 1 g Sat Fat, 0 g Trans Fat, 0 mg Chol, 527 mg Sod, 51 g Carb, 6 g Sugar, 10 g Fib, 11 g Prot, 86 mg Calc.

8 PointsPlus© value

RED BEAN, QUINOA, AND PEPITA SALAD

SERVES 1

- ▲ ¼ cup quinoa, rinsed
- ½ cup plus 1 tablespoon water
- 1 tablespoon lime juice
- ½ teaspoon olive oil
- ½ teaspoon minced chipotles en adobo
- ⅛ teaspoon salt
- ▲ 1 small tomato, diced
- ▲ ⅓ cup canned small red beans, rinsed and drained
- ▲ ¼ cup diced poblano pepper
- 3 tablespoons chopped fresh cilantro
- ▲ 1½ tablespoons chopped red onion
- ▲ 2 cups shredded romaine lettuce
- 1 teaspoon pepitas (toasted pumpkin seeds)

1 Combine quinoa and ½ cup water in small saucepan; bring to boil. Reduce heat and cover. Simmer until liquid is absorbed and quinoa is tender, about 15 minutes. Transfer to plate to cool.

2 Meanwhile, stir together remaining 1 tablespoon water, lime juice, oil, chipotles, and salt in medium bowl. Add tomato, beans, poblano, cilantro, onion, and quinoa; toss to combine. Place lettuce on plate. Top with salad and sprinkle with pepitas.

PER SERVING (1 plate): 359 Cal, 9 g Total Fat, 1 g Sat Fat, 0 g Trans Fat, 0 mg Chol, 424 mg Sod, 59 g Carb, 6 g Sugar, 15 g Fib, 16 g Prot, 109 mg Calc.

STAY ON TRACK

Top the salad with a peeled and sliced Kirby cucumber to add crunch and make the salad even more filling.

CREAMY PASTA, CORN, AND TOMATO SALAD

SERVES 1

▲ 2 **ounces shell-shaped whole wheat pasta**

▲ ½ **cup frozen corn kernels**

1 **tablespoon low-fat mayonnaise**

1 **teaspoon white-wine vinegar**

Pinch salt

Pinch black pepper

▲ 6 **cherry tomatoes, cut in half**

▲ 2 **tablespoons diced red onion**

2 **tablespoons finely shredded Parmesan cheese**

2 **fresh basil leaves, thinly sliced**

1 Cook pasta according to package directions, adding corn during last 2 minutes of cooking. Drain and rinse under cold water until cooled.

2 Meanwhile, stir together mayonnaise, vinegar, salt, and pepper in medium bowl. Add pasta mixture, tomatoes, onion, Parmesan, and basil and toss to coat.

PER SERVING (about 2 cups): 358 Cal, 6 g Total Fat, 3 g Sat Fat, 0 g Trans Fat, 10 mg Chol, 726 mg Sod, 65 g Carb, 8 g Sugar, 8 g Fib, 17 g Prot, 219 mg Calc.

10 PointsPlus© value

TOASTED BULGUR SALAD WITH RICOTTA SALATA

SERVES 1

▲ ¼ **cup bulgur**

¾ **cup water**

½ **teaspoon grated lemon zest**

2 **teaspoons lemon juice**

1 **teaspoon olive oil**

⅛ **teaspoon salt**

Pinch black pepper

▲ ½ **cup grape tomatoes, halved**

▲ ½ **cup diced zucchini**

▲ ¼ **cup diced yellow or orange bell pepper**

▲ ¼ **cup fresh corn kernels**

¼ **cup chopped fresh basil**

1 **tablespoon crumbled ricotta salata cheese**

1 Put bulgur in small dry saucepan and cook over medium heat, stirring often, until bulgur is lightly browned, about 5 minutes. Add water and bring to boil. Reduce heat to low and cover. Simmer until bulgur is tender, about 7 minutes. Transfer to plate to cool.

2 Meanwhile, stir together lemon zest and juice, oil, salt, and black pepper in medium bowl. Add tomatoes, zucchini, bell pepper, corn, basil, and bulgur; toss to combine. Transfer to plate; sprinkle with ricotta salata.

PER SERVING (2 cups): 269 Cal, 9 g Total Fat, 3 g Sat Fat, 0 g Trans Fat, 0 mg Chol, 561 mg Sod, 43 g Carb, 6 g Sugar, 10 g Fib, 10 g Prot, 80 mg Calc.

7 PointsPlus value

THREE-PEA SALAD WITH CREAMY DILL DRESSING

SERVES 1   UNDER 20 MINUTES

▲ 1   **cup sugar snap peas, trimmed (3 ounces)**

▲ ½   **cup frozen green peas**

▲ 1   **tablespoon plain fat-free Greek yogurt**

1   **tablespoon reduced-fat mayonnaise**

1   **tablespoon chopped fresh dill**

2   **teaspoons minced shallot**

2   **teaspoons water**

¼   **teaspoon apple cider vinegar**

Pinch salt

Pinch black pepper

▲ 1   **cup loosely packed pea shoots or watercress, trimmed**

1 Bring small saucepan of water to boil over high heat. Add sugar snap peas and green peas; cook until crisp-tender and bright green, about 1 minute. Drain; then rinse under cold running water to stop cooking. Drain on paper towels.

2 To make dressing, stir together yogurt, mayonnaise, dill, shallot, water, vinegar, salt, and pepper in small bowl.

3 Arrange pea shoots on plate. Top with sugar snap peas and green peas. Drizzle with dressing.

PER SERVING (1 plate): 120 Cal, 2 g Total Fat, 1 g Sat Fat, 0 g Trans Fat, 0 mg Chol, 371 mg Sod, 18 g Carb, 8 g Sugar, 5 g Fib, 7 g Prot, 97 mg Calc.

FOR YOUR INFO

Pea shoots are the delicately flavored leaves and tendrils of young pea plants. Toss them into salads, or use them instead of lettuce in sandwiches.

Any of these salads makes a satisfying summer lunch.

TOASTED BULGUR SALAD WITH RICOTTA SALATA, PAGE 39

THREE-PEA SALAD WITH CREAMY DILL DRESSING

PEAR, ORANGE, AND AVOCADO SALAD WITH PINE NUTS, PAGE 42

PEAR, ORANGE, AND AVOCADO SALAD WITH PINE NUTS

SERVES 1 UNDER 20 MINUTES

- **2** **tablespoons orange juice**
- **1** **tablespoon red-wine vinegar**
- **1** **tablespoon chopped fresh cilantro**
- **1** **teaspoon olive oil**
- **⅛** **teaspoon salt**
- **⅛** **teaspoon black pepper**
- ▲ **1** **navel orange, peeled and cut into segments**
- ▲ **½** **Asian pear, cut into thin strips**
- **⅛** **avocado, peeled and sliced**
- ▲ **2** **cups lightly packed mixed salad greens**
- **1** **teaspoon pine nuts, toasted**

1 Stir together orange juice, vinegar, cilantro, oil, salt, and pepper in medium bowl.

2 Add orange, pear, and avocado; toss to combine. Place salad greens on serving plate. Top with orange mixture and sprinkle with pine nuts.

PER SERVING (1 salad): 219 Cal, 10 g Total Fat, 1 g Sat Fat, 0 g Trans Fat, 0 mg Chol, 335 mg Sod, 35 g Carb, 19 g Sugar, 9 g Fib, 4 g Prot, 71 mg Calc.

FOR YOUR INFO

To toast pine nuts, place them in a small dry skillet over medium-low heat. Cook, shaking pan frequently, until the nuts are lightly browned and fragrant, about 2 minutes.

MANCHEGO, APPLE, AND WALNUT SALAD

SERVES 1 UNDER 20 MINUTES

1½ **teaspoons sherry vinegar**

1 **teaspoon toasted walnut oil**

1 **teaspoon minced shallot**

¼ **teaspoon Dijon mustard**

⅛ **teaspoon salt**

Pinch black pepper

▲ 2 **cups lightly packed baby arugula**

▲ ½ **Gala apple, cored and thinly sliced**

½ **tablespoon chopped walnuts**

1 **tablespoons shaved Manchego cheese**

1 Whisk together vinegar, oil, shallot, mustard, salt, and pepper in medium bowl.

2 Add arugula, apple, walnuts, and Manchego; toss to combine. Serve at once.

PER SERVING (3 cups): 170 Cal, 11 g Total Fat, 3 g Sat Fat, 0 g Trans Fat, 10 mg Chol, 404 mg Sod, 15 g Carb, 10 g Sugar, 3 g Fib, 5 g Prot, 225 mg Calc.

5 PointsPlus® value

CHAPTER 2

FAVORITE PASTAS AND PIZZAS

Solo dinners are a pleasure with dishes as indulgent as these.

GRILLED STEAK WITH THAI-STYLE NOODLE SALAD

SERVES 1   UNDER 20 MINUTES

2   **ounces thin rice noodles**

▲ 2   **radishes, shredded**

▲ 1   **scallion, thinly sliced**

1½   **tablespoons chopped fresh mint**

3   **teaspoons reduced-sodium soy sauce**

1   **teaspoon Asian (dark) sesame oil**

▲ 1   **(¼-pound) lean filet mignon steak, trimmed**

1   **tablespoon Thai peanut sauce**

1 Place noodles in medium bowl; cover with boiling water. Let stand until noodles soften, about 3 minutes. Drain, rinse under cold running water, and return to bowl. Add radishes, scallion, mint, 2 teaspoons soy sauce, and ½ teaspoon oil; toss to coat.

2 Spray ridged cast-iron grill skillet with nonstick spray and set over medium-high heat. Combine remaining 1 teaspoon soy sauce and remaining ½ teaspoon oil on small plate; add steak and turn to coat. Add beef to skillet and cook, turning once, until instant-read thermometer inserted into side of steak registers 145°F for medium, about 6 minutes.

3 To serve, place noodle salad on plate. Top salad with steak and drizzle with peanut sauce.

PER SERVING (1 plate): 454 Cal, 14 g Total Fat, 4 g Sat Fat, 0 g Trans Fat, 67 mg Chol, 877 mg Sod, 54 g Carb, 1 g Sugar, 1 g Fib, 27 g Prot, 54 mg Calc.

12 PointsPlus® value

DOUBLE IT   To make the recipe for two, use 2 (¼-pound) lean filet mignon steaks and double all the remaining ingredients.

BEEF BOLOGNESE WITH EGGPLANT

SERVES 1

- ▲ ¼ **pound lean ground beef (7% fat or less)**
- ▲ ¼ **cup chopped onion**
- 1 **small garlic clove, minced**
- ▲ 1 **small eggplant (½ pound), peeled and chopped**
- ▲ ½ **cup canned tomato sauce**
- 3 **tablespoons water**
- **Pinch black pepper**
- 2 **tablespoons chopped fresh basil**
- ▲ 2 **ounces whole wheat rigatoni**
- 1 **tablespoon grated Parmesan**

1 Spray medium skillet with nonstick spray and set over medium heat. Add beef, onion, and garlic, and cook, breaking up beef with wooden spoon, until beef is browned, 5 minutes. Add eggplant, tomato sauce, water, and pepper. Cover skillet and cook, stirring occasionally, until eggplant is tender, 12–15 minutes. Stir in basil.

2 Meanwhile, cook rigatoni according to package directions, omitting salt if desired.

3 Transfer rigatoni to serving bowl. Top with sauce and sprinkle with Parmesan.

PER SERVING (scant 2 cups pasta and sauce): 523 Cal, 10 g Total Fat, 4 g Sat Fat, 0 g Trans Fat, 69 mg Chol, 829 mg Sod, 74 g Carb, 17 g Sugar, 15 g Fib, 39 g Prot, 191 mg Calc.

STAY ON TRACK

Make the sauce chunkier and more filling by adding a chopped plum tomato when you add the eggplant in step 1.

ASIAN STEAK STIR-FRY WITH SESAME SOBA NOODLES

SERVES 1   UNDER 20 MINUTES

▲ 2   **ounces 100% buckwheat soba noodles**

½   **teaspoon Asian (dark) sesame oil**

½   **teaspoon sesame seeds**

½   **teaspoon canola oil**

▲ 1   **(¼-pound) piece lean sirloin steak, trimmed and thinly sliced**

▲ 1   **small red bell pepper, thinly sliced**

1   **small garlic clove, minced**

½   **teaspoon sugar**

½   **teaspoon black pepper**

▲ 1   **tablespoon reduced-sodium chicken broth**

2   **teaspoons reduced-sodium soy sauce**

1 Cook noodles according to package directions; drain and transfer to small bowl. Stir in sesame oil and sesame seeds; toss to coat.

2 Meanwhile, heat canola oil in medium nonstick skillet over medium heat. Add steak and stir-fry until lightly browned, about 4 minutes.

3 Add bell pepper and garlic; stir-fry until crisp-tender, 2 minutes. Add sugar and black pepper. Cook, stirring constantly, until sugar begins to melt and caramelize, about 2 minutes. Stir in broth and soy sauce, scraping up browned bits from bottom of skillet.

4 Place noodles on plate; top with steak mixture.

PER SERVING (2 cups): 448 Cal, 12 g Total Fat, 2 g Sat Fat, 0 g Trans Fat, 49 mg Chol, 426 mg Sod, 52 g Carb, 7 g Sugar, 5 g Fib, 34 g Prot, 50 mg Calc.

FOR YOUR INFO

Look for soba noodles that are made with 100% buckwheat flour. Many brands combine buckwheat flour with white flour, resulting in noodles with less whole grain and fiber.

Try this stir-fry with broccoli instead of bell peppers.
ASIAN STEAK STIR-FRY WITH SESAME SOBA NOODLES

PENNE WITH SAUSAGE, ZUCCHINI, TOMATOES, AND RICOTTA

SERVES 1

- ▲ 2 **ounces whole wheat penne**
- 2 **ounces Italian-style sausage, casing removed**
- ▲ ¼ **cup diced onion**
- 1 **small garlic clove, minced**
- ▲ 1 **small zucchini, diced**
- ▲ 6 **cherry tomatoes, halved**
- 2 **tablespoons minced fresh basil**
- 2 **tablespoons part-skim ricotta**

1 Cook penne according to package directions, omitting salt if desired.

2 Meanwhile, add sausage, onion, and garlic to medium nonstick skillet. Set over medium heat and cook, stirring with wooden spoon to break up sausage, until browned, about 5 minutes.

3 Add zucchini, tomatoes, and basil. Cook, stirring often, until zucchini is crisp-tender, 2 minutes. Add pasta and stir to combine. Transfer to plate; top with ricotta.

PER SERVING (1 ⅔ cups): 401 Cal, 11 g Total Fat, 4 g Sat Fat, 0 g Trans Fat, 24 mg Chol, 406 mg Sod, 58 g Carb, 10 g Sugar, 8 g Fib, 18 g Prot, 128 mg Calc.

10 PointsPlus® value

STAY ON TRACK — Make this dish more colorful and filling by adding ½ of a yellow or red bell pepper, chopped, along with the sausage in step 2.

CHICKEN AND NOODLE STIR-FRY WITH AVOCADO AND CILANTRO

SERVES 1   UNDER 20 MINUTES

2   **ounces wide rice noodles**

▲ 2   **tablespoons reduced-sodium chicken broth**

1   **tablespoon reduced-sodium soy sauce**

2   **teaspoons lime juice**

½   **teaspoon cornstarch**

1   **teaspoon canola oil**

▲ 1   **(¼-pound) skinless boneless chicken breast, thinly sliced**

2   **teaspoons minced peeled fresh ginger**

1   **small garlic clove, minced**

▲ 1   **small yellow bell pepper, thinly sliced**

▲ 2   **scallions, thinly sliced**

¼   **avocado, peeled and diced**

2   **tablespoons minced fresh cilantro**

1   Place noodles in medium bowl; cover with boiling water. Let stand until noodles soften, about 5 minutes. Drain and set aside.

2   Meanwhile, whisk together broth, soy sauce, lime juice, and cornstarch in small bowl.

3   Heat oil in medium nonstick skillet over medium heat. Add chicken, ginger, and garlic; stir-fry until chicken is lightly browned, about 3 minutes. Add bell pepper and scallions; stir-fry until vegetables are crisp-tender, 2 minutes.

4   Add noodles; stir-fry 1 minute. Stir broth mixture and add to skillet. Stir-fry until mixture is bubbling and thickened, about 1 minute. Remove from heat. Add avocado and cilantro; toss to combine.

PER SERVING (2 cups): 507 Cal, 13 g Total Fat, 2 g Sat Fat, 0 g Trans Fat, 63 mg Chol, 615 mg Sod, 71 g Carb, 6 g Sugar, 5 g Fib, 28 g Prot, 83 mg Calc.

13 PointsPlus® value

CHICKEN AND BOW TIES WITH ARUGULA

SERVES 1

▲ 2 **ounces whole wheat farfalle (bow ties)**

½ **teaspoon canola oil**

▲ 1 **(¼-pound) skinless boneless chicken breast, thinly sliced**

⅛ **teaspoon salt**

⅛ **teaspoon black pepper**

½ **teaspoon minced garlic**

▲ 1 **cup cherry tomatoes, halved**

▲ 1 **cup packed baby arugula**

½ **teaspoon grated lemon zest**

2 **teaspoons lemon juice**

1 **tablespoon crumbled goat cheese**

1 Cook farfalle according to package directions, omitting salt if desired.

2 Meanwhile, heat oil in medium nonstick skillet over medium heat. Sprinkle chicken with salt and pepper; add to skillet. Cook, stirring often, until chicken is lightly browned, about 4 minutes.

3 Add garlic and cook, stirring constantly until fragrant, 1 minute. Add tomatoes and cook until heated through, about 2 minutes. Add pasta, arugula, and lemon zest and juice. Cook, stirring constantly, until arugula begins to wilt, about 1 minute. Transfer to plate; sprinkle with goat cheese.

PER SERVING (2 cups): 430 Cal, 10 g Total Fat, 3 g Sat Fat, 0 g Trans Fat, 69 mg Chol, 421 mg Sod, 51 g Carb, 7 g Sugar, 7 g Fib, 35 g Prot, 104 mg Calc.

STAY ON TRACK — Pump up the veggies in this dish by adding 1 cup of thinly sliced zucchini to the pasta cooking water for the last 2 minutes of cooking in step 1.

Cherry tomatoes give this dish a flavor boost.
CHICKEN AND BOW TIES WITH ARUGULA

CHICKEN AND FUSILLI WITH FETA AND MINT

SERVES 1

▲ 2 **ounces whole wheat fusilli**

1 **teaspoon canola oil**

▲ 1 **(¼-pound) skinless boneless chicken breast, thinly sliced**

▲ 1 **small yellow bell pepper, thinly sliced**

▲ ½ **small red onion, thinly sliced**

▲ ½ **jalapeño pepper, seeded and minced**

½ **teaspoon minced garlic**

½ **teaspoon grated lime zest**

1½ **tablespoons lime juice**

⅛ **teaspoon salt**

1 **tablespoon minced fresh mint**

1 **tablespoon crumbled feta cheese**

1 Cook fusilli according to package directions, omitting salt if desired.

2 Heat oil in medium nonstick skillet over medium heat. Add chicken and cook, stirring often, until browned and cooked through, about 4 minutes. Transfer to plate. Add bell pepper, onion, jalapeño, and garlic to skillet. Cook, stirring often, until vegetables are crisp-tender, about 3 minutes.

3 Add chicken, pasta, lime zest and juice, and salt to skillet; toss to combine. Remove from heat; stir in mint. Transfer to plate; sprinkle with feta.

PER SERVING (1 ⅔ cups): 476 Cal, 11 g Total Fat, 3 g Sat Fat, 0 g Trans Fat, 71 mg Chol, 466 mg Sod, 61 g Carb, 9 g Sugar, 8 g Fib, 34 g Prot, 118 mg Calc.

STAY ON TRACK

To add more color and flavor to this dish, add ½ cup halved grape tomatoes when you add the chicken in step 3.

SZECHUAN-STYLE TURKEY WITH NOODLES

SERVES 1   UNDER 20 MINUTES

2   **ounces thin rice noodles**

1   **teaspoon Asian (dark) sesame oil**

▲ 2   **scallions, thinly sliced**

1   **tablespoon minced peeled fresh ginger**

1   **small garlic clove, minced**

½   **teaspoon red pepper flakes**

▲ 4   **ounces ground skinless turkey breast**

1   **tablespoon reduced-sodium soy sauce**

1   **tablespoon rice vinegar**

1   **tablespoon chopped fresh cilantro**

1 Place noodles in medium bowl; cover with boiling water. Let stand until noodles soften, about 3 minutes. Drain and set aside.

2 Meanwhile, heat oil in medium nonstick skillet over medium heat. Add scallions, ginger, garlic, and pepper flakes; cook, stirring constantly until fragrant, 1 minute.

3 Add turkey. Cook, breaking turkey apart with wooden spoon, until no longer pink, about 5 minutes. Stir in soy sauce and vinegar. Add noodles; toss to combine. Transfer to plate; sprinkle with cilantro.

PER SERVING (1 ⅓ cups): 389 Cal, 6 g Total Fat, 1 g Sat Fat, 0 g Trans Fat, 45 mg Chol, 611 mg Sod, 55 g Carb, 1 g Sugar, 2 g Fib, 30 g Prot, 46 mg Calc.

FOR YOUR INFO Look for ground skinless turkey breast rather than products labeled "ground turkey." Ground turkey contains white and dark meat turkey, and it may contain skin.

TURKEY WITH FETTUCCINE AND FRESH TOMATO SAUCE

SERVES 1   UNDER 20 MINUTES

- ▲ 2   **ounces whole wheat fettuccine**
- ▲ 1   **(¼-pound) turkey cutlet**
- 2   **pinches salt**
- 2   **pinches black pepper**
- 1   **teaspoon olive oil**
- ▲ 2   **tablespoons diced onion**
- ▲ 1   **large tomato, chopped**
- ¼   **cup dry white wine**
- 1   **small garlic clove, minced**
- 1   **tablespoon chopped fresh basil or ½ teaspoon dried**
- 1   **tablespoon grated Parmesan cheese**

1 Cook fettuccine according to package directions, omitting salt if desired.

2 Meanwhile, spray medium skillet with nonstick spray and set over medium heat. Sprinkle turkey with pinch of salt and pinch of pepper and add to skillet. Cook until turkey is lightly browned and cooked through, 2–3 minutes on each side. Transfer turkey to plate. Cover to keep warm.

3 Add oil to skillet. Add onion and cook, stirring often, until softened, 3 minutes. Add tomato, wine, garlic, and pinch of salt and pinch of pepper. Cook, stirring occasionally, until sauce is slightly thickened, 4–5 minutes. Stir in basil.

4 Place pasta on plate. Top with turkey and spoon sauce over turkey. Sprinkle with Parmesan.

PER SERVING (1 turkey cutlet with about 1 cup pasta and ½ cup sauce): 469 Cal, 8 g Total Fat, 2 g Sat Fat, 0 g Trans Fat, 49 mg Chol, 482 mg Sod, 52 g Carb, 7 g Sugar, 10 g Fib, 40 g Prot, 112 mg Calc.

11 PointsPlus© value

TURKEY SAUSAGE, APPLE, AND ORZO PILAF

SERVES 1

2½ teaspoons olive oil

3 ounces sweet Italian-style turkey sausage, casing removed

▲ 1 small apple, peeled, cored, and thinly sliced

▲ 2 scallions, thinly sliced

2 teaspoons minced fresh sage

▲ ½ cup reduced-sodium chicken broth

▲ ⅓ cup whole wheat orzo

1 Heat oil in medium nonstick skillet over medium heat. Add sausage and cook, breaking apart sausage with wooden spoon until no longer pink, about 4 minutes.

2 Add apple, scallions, and sage. Cook, stirring often, until scallions soften, about 2 minutes. Add broth and orzo; bring to boil. Reduce heat, cover, and simmer until orzo is tender, about 8 minutes. Remove from heat and let stand, covered, 3 minutes.

PER SERVING (1 ¾ cups): 442 Cal, 14 g Total Fat, 1 g Sat Fat, 0 g Trans Fat, 51 mg Chol, 589 mg Sod, 59 g Carb, 17 g Sugar, 10 g Fib, 26 g Prot, 43 mg Calc.

DOUBLE IT
To make the pilaf for two, double all the ingredients except the sage; use 1 tablespoon minced fresh sage.

*Fresh fennel gives the salsa
a delicate anise flavor.*
**SALMON AND SWISS CHARD
WITH TOMATO-FENNEL SALSA**

SALMON AND SWISS CHARD WITH TOMATO-FENNEL SALSA

SERVES 1

1   (¼-pound) skinless salmon fillet

½   teaspoon fennel seeds, crushed

3   pinches salt

3   pinches black pepper

½   teaspoon olive oil

1   small garlic clove, minced

▲ 4   large Swiss chard leaves, trimmed and thinly sliced

▲ 2   tablespoons diced red bell pepper

▲ ¼   cup reduced-sodium chicken broth

▲ ½   cup grape tomatoes, quartered

▲ ¼   cup fresh diced fennel bulb

1   tablespoon minced fresh fennel fronds or flat-leaf parsley

1   teaspoon grated lemon zest

2   teaspoons lemon juice

1 Preheat broiler. Spray small baking pan with nonstick spray.

2 Sprinkle salmon with fennel seeds, pinch of salt, and pinch of pepper; place in prepared baking pan. Broil, 5 inches from heat, until salmon is just opaque in center, about 8 minutes.

3 Meanwhile, heat oil in medium skillet over medium-high heat. Add garlic; cook, stirring constantly, until fragrant, 30 seconds. Add Swiss chard, bell pepper, and broth; partially cover and cook, stirring occasionally, until chard is tender and most of liquid is evaporated, about 6 minutes. Stir in pinch of salt and pinch of pepper.

4 To make salsa, stir together tomatoes, fennel bulb, fennel fronds, lemon zest and juice, and pinch of salt and pinch of pepper in small bowl.

5 Transfer chard mixture to serving plate; top with salmon. Spoon salsa over salmon and Swiss chard.

PER SERVING (1 salmon fillet, about ½ cup Swiss chard, and ¾ cup salsa): 253 Cal, 13 g Total Fat, 3 g Sat Fat, 0 g Trans Fat, 54 mg Chol, 585 mg Sod, 12 g Carb, 4 g Sugar, 4 g Fib, 23 g Prot, 96 mg Calc.

6 PointsPlus® value

STAY ON TRACK

Serve the salmon with spinach linguine (⅔ cup cooked spinach linguine per serving will increase the **PointsPlus** value by **3**).

SMOKY SHRIMP AND ROASTED RED PEPPER WITH LINGUINE

SERVES 1

▲ 2 **ounces whole wheat linguine**

1 **teaspoon olive oil**

▲ ¼ **cup minced onion**

1 **small garlic clove, minced**

¼ **teaspoon red pepper flakes**

▲ ¼ **pound medium peeled and deveined shrimp**

▲ ½ **cup thinly sliced roasted red bell pepper (not oil-packed)**

1 **teaspoon smoked paprika**

Pinch salt

1 **teaspoon grated lemon zest**

2 **teaspoons lemon juice**

1 **tablespoon chopped fresh flat-leaf parsley**

1 **tablespoon grated Parmesan cheese**

1 Cook linguine according to package directions, omitting salt if desired.

2 Meanwhile, heat oil in medium nonstick skillet over medium heat. Add onion, garlic, and pepper flakes; cook, stirring often, until onion softens, about 3 minutes.

3 Add shrimp; cook, stirring often, 2 minutes. Add bell pepper, paprika, and salt. Cook, stirring constantly, until shrimp are just opaque in center, about 2 minutes longer.

4 Add linguine, lemon zest and juice, and parsley; stir to combine. Transfer to plate; sprinkle with Parmesan.

PER SERVING (1 ¾ cups): 423 Cal, 9 g Total Fat, 2 g Sat Fat, 0 g Trans Fat, 226 mg Chol, 693 mg Sod, 53 g Carb, 6 g Sugar, 10 g Fib, 36 g Prot, 157 mg Calc.

FOR YOUR INFO

When you only need a small amount of onion, mince the whole onion and place the remainder in a small zip-close plastic bag. Pop it in the freezer to use another time.

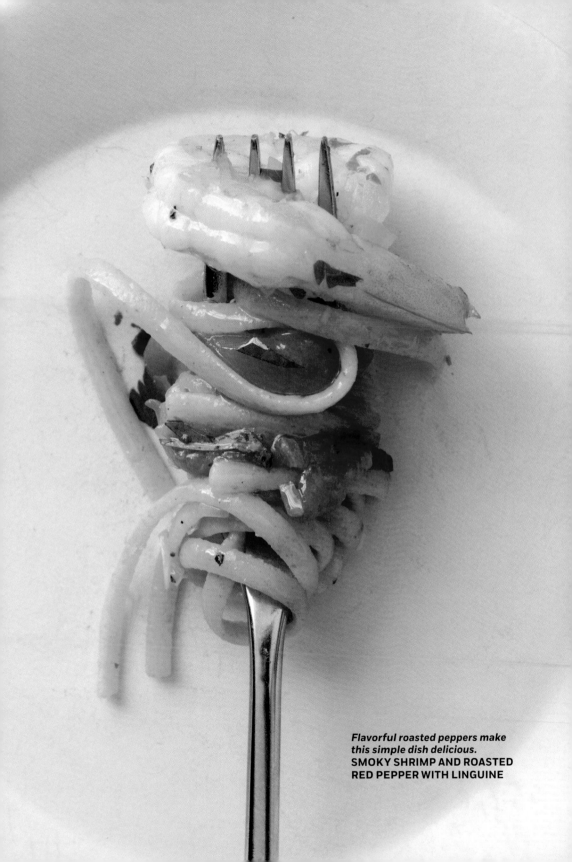

Flavorful roasted peppers make this simple dish delicious.
SMOKY SHRIMP AND ROASTED RED PEPPER WITH LINGUINE

SHRIMP AND PASTA WITH SWISS CHARD

SERVES 1

- ▲ 2 **ounces whole wheat rotini**
- 1 **teaspoon olive oil**
- 1 **small garlic clove, minced**
- ¼ **teaspoon red pepper flakes**
- ▲ ¼ **pound medium peeled and deveined shrimp**
- ▲ 1 **cup chopped Swiss chard leaves**
- ▲ 1 **small tomato, chopped**
- 2 **tablespoons dry white wine**
  Pinch salt
- 1 **tablespoon grated pecorino Romano cheese**

1 Cook rotini according to package directions, omitting salt if desired.

2 Heat oil in medium nonstick skillet over medium heat. Add garlic and pepper flakes; cook, stirring constantly, until fragrant, 1 minute. Add shrimp; cook, stirring often, 2 minutes.

3 Add Swiss chard and tomato; cook, stirring constantly, until chard wilts, about 1 minute. Add pasta, wine, and salt. Cook, stirring constantly, until most of liquid evaporates, 1 minute. Transfer to plate; sprinkle with pecorino.

PER SERVING (2 cups): 381 Cal, 9 g Total Fat, 2 g Sat Fat, 0 g Trans Fat, 8 mg Chol, 370 mg Sod, 59 g Carb, 5 g Sugar, 8 g Fib, 14 g Prot, 198 mg Calc.

MUSHROOM-LEEK FETTUCCINI WITH PECANS AND GOAT CHEESE

SERVES 1

- ▲ 2 **ounces whole wheat fettuccini**
- 1 **teaspoon unsalted butter**
- ▲ ¾ **cup sliced cremini mushrooms**
- ▲ ½ **cup thinly sliced leek, pale green and white parts only**
- ¼ **cup dry white wine**
- 1½ **teaspoons minced fresh thyme or ½ teaspoon dried**
- ⅛ **teaspoon salt**
- 1 **tablespoon crumbled goat cheese**
- 1 **teaspoon chopped pecans**

1 Cook fettuccine according to package directions, omitting salt if desired.

2 Heat butter in medium nonstick skillet over medium heat. Add mushrooms and leek. Cook, stirring often, until vegetables soften, about 5 minutes. Add wine, thyme, and salt. Reduce heat to low, cover, and simmer until vegetables are tender, about 5 minutes longer.

3 Add pasta and cook, stirring constantly, until most of liquid evaporates, about 1 minute. Transfer to plate; sprinkle with goat cheese and pecans.

PER SERVING (1 ⅔ cups): 377 Cal, 9 g Total Fat, 5 g Sat Fat, 0 g Trans Fat, 17 mg Chol, 360 mg Sod, 53 g Carb, 5 g Sugar, 9 g Fib, 13 g Prot, 86 mg Calc.

9 PointsPlus value

GRUYÈRE-SPINACH LASAGNA

SERVES 1

▲ 1 **whole wheat lasagna noodle**

1 **cup low-fat (1%) milk**

2 **teaspoons all-purpose flour**

2 **tablespoons shredded Gruyère cheese**

¼ **teaspoon dried thyme**

2 **pinches salt**

Pinch ground nutmeg

1 **teaspoon olive oil**

1 **garlic clove, minced**

▲ 2 **cups loosely packed baby spinach**

▲ 1 **plum tomato, chopped**

1 **tablespoon finely grated Parmesan cheese**

1 Cook lasagna according to package directions, omitting salt if desired.

2 Preheat broiler. Spray small (8-ounce) flameproof casserole or gratin dish with nonstick spray.

3 Meanwhile, to make sauce, whisk together milk and flour in small saucepan until smooth. Cook over medium heat, whisking constantly, until mixture comes to boil and thickens, about 5 minutes. Remove from heat. Add Gruyère, thyme, 1 pinch salt, and nutmeg. Whisk until cheese is melted. Set aside.

4 Heat oil in medium skillet over medium heat. Add garlic and cook, stirring constantly, until fragrant, 1 minute. Add spinach and remaining pinch of salt; cook, stirring constantly, until spinach is wilted, about 1 minute. Transfer to plate.

5 Cut lasagna noodle into 3 equal pieces. Place 1 piece of noodle in prepared casserole dish. Top with half of spinach mixture and half of tomato; then ⅓ cup sauce. Repeat layering with 1 piece of noodle, remaining spinach mixture, remaining tomato, and ⅓ cup of remaining sauce. Top with remaining piece of noodle and remaining sauce. Sprinkle with Parmesan.

6 Broil 5 inches from broiler until sauce is bubbling and cheese is lightly browned, about 2 minutes.

PER SERVING (1 piece lasagna): 361 Cal, 14 g Total Fat, 6 g Sat Fat, 0 g Trans Fat, 31 mg Chol, 603 mg Sod, 41 g Carb, 14 g Sugar, 7 g Fib, 20 g Prot, 529 mg Calc.

This recipe makes it easy to make lasagna for one.
GRUYÈRE-SPINACH LASAGNA

LEMON LINGUINE WITH ASPARAGUS, BASIL, AND PISTACHIOS

SERVES 1

▲ 2 **ounces whole wheat linguine**

1 **teaspoon olive oil**

▲ 6 **asparagus spears, trimmed and cut into 1-inch pieces**

2 **tablespoons minced shallot**

▲ 3 **tablespoons reduced-sodium vegetable broth**

2 **tablespoons half-and-half**

2 **tablespoons minced fresh basil**

1½ **teaspoons grated lemon zest**

⅛ **teaspoon salt**

1 **tablespoon shaved Parmesan cheese**

1 **teaspoon chopped unsalted pistachios**

1 Cook linguine according to package directions, omitting salt if desired.

2 Heat oil in medium nonstick skillet over medium heat. Add asparagus and shallot; cook, stirring often, until asparagus is crisp-tender, about 4 minutes.

3 Add broth and half-and-half; bring to simmer and cook 1 minute. Add pasta, basil, lemon zest, and salt. Cook, stirring constantly, 1 minute. Transfer to plate. Top with Parmesan and pistachios.

PER SERVING (2 cups): 356 Cal, 11 g Total Fat, 4 g Sat Fat, 0 g Trans Fat, 19 mg Chol, 424 mg Sod, 54 g Carb, 7 g Sugar, 10 g Fib, 15 g Prot, 177 mg Calc.

9 PointsPlus® value

MOROCCAN LAMB AND FETA PIZZA

SERVES 1

- **3** ounces lean ground lamb
- **½** teaspoon cinnamon
- **½** teaspoon ground coriander
- **½** teaspoon ground cumin
- **½** teaspoon ground ginger
- **⅛** teaspoon salt
- **1** (9 x 5-inch) whole wheat lavash
- **1½** teaspoons pomegranate molasses
- ▲ **1** plum tomato, thinly sliced
- **2** tablespoons crumbled feta cheese
- **2** teaspoons fresh chopped mint

1 Preheat oven to 375°F. Spray large baking sheet with nonstick spray.

2 Place lamb in medium nonstick skillet and set over medium heat. Cook, breaking apart lamb with wooden spoon, until lightly browned, about 4 minutes. Stir in cinnamon, coriander, cumin, ginger, and salt.

3 Place lavash on prepared baking sheet. Spread molasses to edge of lavash. Top with lamb mixture; then with tomato. Sprinkle with feta.

4 Bake until cheese is melted and lavash is lightly browned, about 12 minutes. Sprinkle with mint. Cut into slices to serve.

PER SERVING (1 pizza): 455 Cal, 12 g Total Fat, 5 g Sat Fat, 0 g Trans Fat, 81 mg Chol, 844 mg Sod, 51 g Carb, 8 g Sugar, 5 g Fib, 31 g Prot, 192 mg Calc.

FOR YOUR INFO

Pomegranate molasses is a tart-sweet syrup made by boiling down pomegranate juice. Use it in salad dressings and drinks, or drizzle over steamed vegetables and desserts.

Thai peanut sauce pumps up the flavor of this pizza.
THAI CHICKEN AND VEGGIE PIZZA

THAI CHICKEN AND VEGGIE PIZZA

SERVES 1

1 **(6-inch) prebaked whole wheat pizza crust**

1 **tablespoon Thai peanut sauce**

▲ 2 **ounces shredded cooked skinless boneless chicken breast**

▲ 1 **large cremini mushroom, thinly sliced**

▲ 3 **tablespoons minced red bell pepper**

▲ 1 **tablespoon minced red onion**

1 **tablespoon finely shredded Jarlsberg cheese**

1 Preheat oven to 400°F.

2 Place crust on small baking sheet. Spread peanut sauce on crust, leaving ½-inch border around edge. Top with chicken, mushroom, bell pepper, and onion. Sprinkle with Jarlsberg.

3 Bake until cheese is melted and crust is crisp, about 15 minutes.

PER SERVING (1 individual pizza): 408 Cal, 11 g Total Fat, 3 g Sat Fat, 0 g Trans Fat, 57 mg Chol, 787 mg Sod, 45 g Carb, 2 g Sugar, 6 g Fib, 30 g Prot, 171 mg Calc.

SUMMER GARDEN PIZZA

SERVES 1

1	**(6-inch) whole wheat pita bread**
2	**tablespoons pizza sauce**
▲ 3	**tablespoons diced red bell pepper**
▲ 3	**tablespoons thawed frozen corn kernels**
▲ 3	**tablespoons seeded and diced tomato**
▲ 2	**tablespoons diced red onion**
2	**tablespoons minced fresh basil**
3	**tablespoons shredded part-skim mozzarella**
2	**teaspoons balsamic vinegar**

1 Preheat oven to 400°F.

2 Spread one side of pita with pizza sauce; place on small baking sheet. Top with bell pepper, corn, tomato, onion, and basil. Sprinkle with mozzarella.

3 Bake until heated through, about 15 minutes. Drizzle with balsamic vinegar and serve at once.

PER SERVING (1 individual pizza): 301 Cal, 6 g Total Fat, 2 g Sat Fat, 0 g Trans Fat, 11 mg Chol, 641 mg Sod, 51 g Carb, 6 g Sugar, 7 g Fib, 15 g Prot, 331 mg Calc.

FOR YOUR INFO Balsamic vinegar can brighten the flavors of all kinds of foods—like this pizza! Drizzle it on grilled fish or vegetables, or over a steak.

MANCHEGO AND SUNDRIED TOMATO PIZZA

SERVES 1

---

4   **sundried tomatoes (not oil-packed)**

1   **garlic clove, chopped**

2   **teaspoons minced fresh oregano or ½ teaspoon dried**

1   **(6-inch) prebaked whole wheat pizza crust**

3   **tablespoons sliced black olives**

2   **tablespoons shredded Manchego cheese**

1   Place tomatoes in small bowl; cover with boiling water. Let stand until softened, 20 minutes. Drain, reserving soaking water.

2   Preheat oven to 400°F.

3   Place tomatoes in mini–food processor; add garlic, oregano, and 2 tablespoons soaking water. Puree, adding additional soaking water one tablespoon at a time if necessary.

4   Place crust on small baking sheet. Spread tomato mixture on crust, leaving ½-inch border around edge. Top with olives and Manchego.

5   Bake until cheese is melted and crust is crisp, about 15 minutes.

PER SERVING (1 individual pizza): 357 Cal, 12 g Total Fat, 5 g Sat Fat, 0 g Trans Fat, 20 mg Chol, 890 mg Sod, 47 g Carb, 3 g Sugar, 7 g Fib, 15 g Prot, 378 mg Calc.

9 PointsPlus® value

FOR YOUR INFO

Manchego is a Spanish cheese that gets its name from Manchega, the breed of sheep whose milk is used to make the cheese. It has a butterlike texture and a nutty flavor.

WINTER SQUASH, SWISS CHARD, AND ASIAGO PIZZA

SERVES 1

1 teaspoon olive oil

½ teaspoon minced garlic

¼ teaspoon red pepper flakes

▲ 1½ cups chopped Swiss chard leaves

▲ 2 tablespoons reduced-sodium vegetable broth

▲ ⅓ cup thawed frozen squash puree

⅛ teaspoon ground nutmeg

⅛ teaspoon salt

⅛ teaspoon black pepper

1 (6-inch) prebaked whole wheat pizza crust

2 tablespoons shredded Asiago cheese

1 Preheat oven to 400°F.

2 Heat oil in medium nonstick skillet over medium heat. Add garlic and pepper flakes; cook, stirring constantly until fragrant, 1 minute. Add Swiss chard; cook, stirring constantly, until wilted, about 1 minute. Add broth. Cook, stirring often, until chard is tender and liquid has evaporated, about 2 minutes. Set aside.

3 Stir together squash, nutmeg, salt, and pepper in small bowl. Place pizza crust on small baking sheet. Spread squash mixture on crust, leaving ½-inch border around edge. Top with chard mixture; sprinkle with Asiago.

4 Bake until cheese is melted and crust is crisp, about 15 minutes.

PER SERVING (1 individual pizza): 358 Cal, 12 g Total Fat, 3 g Sat Fat, 0 g Trans Fat, 13 mg Chol, 957 mg Sod, 52 g Carb, 1 g Sugar, 9 g Fib, 12 g Prot, 183 mg Calc.

FOR YOUR INFO

Save yourself substantial prep time by keeping a box of frozen squash puree on hand. Use it to make soup or substitute it in recipes that call for canned pumpkin.

Get your veggies in a delicious autumn-inspired pizza.
WINTER SQUASH, SWISS CHARD, AND ASIAGO PIZZA

GOAT CHEESE AND RED GRAPE PIZZA

SERVES 1

2 **ounces soft goat cheese**

1 **teaspoon grated lemon zest**

2 **ounces fresh or thawed frozen whole wheat pizza dough**

▲ 6 **large red seedless grapes, halved**

1 **teaspoon minced fresh rosemary**

1 Preheat oven to 400°F. Spray small baking sheet with nonstick spray.

2 Stir together goat cheese and lemon zest in small bowl. Place dough on prepared baking sheet and press into 6-inch circle. Spread goat cheese mixture on dough, leaving ½-inch border around edge. Top with grapes and rosemary.

3 Bake until crust is crisp, about 17 minutes.

PER SERVING (1 individual pizza): 300 Cal, 14 g Total Fat, 8 g Sat Fat, 0 g Trans Fat, 26 mg Chol, 448 mg Sod, 29 g Carb, 4 g Sugar, 4 g Fib, 15 g Prot, 107 mg Calc.

8 PointsPlus® value

DOUBLE IT

To make pizzas for two, use 2 (2-ounce) pieces of dough, double all the remaining ingredients, and use a medium baking sheet.

CORN AND BLACK BEAN TORTILLA PIZZA

SERVES 1

- **1** **(8-inch) whole-wheat tortilla**
- ▲ **¼** **cup thawed frozen corn kernels**
- ▲ **2** **tablespoons diced red bell pepper**
- ▲ **2** **tablespoons diced onion**
- ▲ **¼** **cup canned black beans, rinsed and drained**
- **⅛** **teaspoon ground cumin**
- **⅛** **teaspoon minced chipotle en adobo**
- ▲ **3** **tablespoons fat-free salsa, drained**
- **¼** **cup shredded reduced-fat Mexican cheese blend**
- **2** **teaspoons chopped fresh cilantro**

1 Preheat oven to 350°F. Spray small baking sheet with nonstick spray. Place tortilla on baking sheet and bake until crisp, 8–10 minutes.

2 Meanwhile, spray small skillet with nonstick spray and set over medium heat. Add corn, bell pepper, and onion. Cook, stirring occasionally, until vegetables are softened, 5 minutes. Add beans, cumin, and chipotles and cook, stirring constantly, until heated through, 2 minutes.

3 Spread salsa over tortilla. Top with corn mixture; sprinkle with cheese. Return tortilla to oven and bake until cheese melts, about 4 minutes. Sprinkle with cilantro and serve at once.

PER SERVING (1 individual pizza): 277 Cal, 8 g Total Fat, 4 g Sat Fat, 0 g Trans Fat, 17 mg Chol, 890 mg Sod, 37 g Carb, 6 g Sugar, 6 g Fib, 14 g Prot, 352 mg Calc.

7 PointsPlus® value

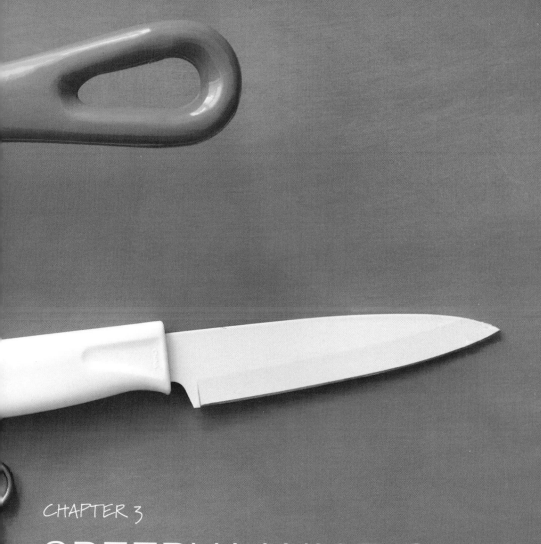

CHAPTER 3

SPEEDY MAIN DISHES

You've always got time to make a satisfying
dinner with these easy one-pan meals.

FILET MIGNON WITH MINTY LENTILS

SERVES 1 UNDER 20 MINUTES

▲ 1 (¼-pound) lean filet mignon steak, trimmed

⅛ teaspoon salt

⅛ teaspoon black pepper

1 teaspoon olive oil

▲ ⅓ cup precooked green (French) lentils

▲ ⅓ cup quartered precooked beets, red and/or yellow

▲ ¼ cup thinly sliced roasted red bell pepper (not oil-packed)

▲ 1 cup baby spinach

1 tablespoon chopped fresh mint

1 Sprinkle steak with salt and black pepper. Heat ½ teaspoon oil in small skillet over medium-high heat. Add steak and cook, turning once, until instant-read thermometer inserted into side of steak registers 145°F for medium-rare, 6–8 minutes. Transfer to plate and keep warm.

2 Reduce heat to medium. Add remaining ½ teaspoon oil to same skillet. Add lentils, beets, and bell pepper. Cook, stirring often, until heated through, about 1 minute. Add spinach and cook, stirring often, just until wilted, about 1 minute. Remove from heat; stir in mint. Serve steak with lentils.

PER SERVING (1 filet mignon and 1 cup lentils): 332 Cal, 12 g Total Fat, 3 g Sat Fat, 0 g Trans Fat, 67 mg Chol, 822 mg Sod, 24 g Carb, 7 g Sugar, 9 g Fib, 32 g Prot, 73 mg Calc.

Precooked lentils are available in vacuum-sealed packages in many supermarkets or you can make your own by simmering dried lentils in water until tender, about 25 minutes.

Veggie-packed lentils are the perfect partner for steak.
FILET MIGNON WITH MINTY LENTILS

PEPPERCORN-CRUSTED FILET MIGNON WITH PORT WINE SAUCE

SERVES 1   UNDER 20 MINUTES

▲ 1   **(¼-pound) lean filet mignon steak, trimmed**

½   **teaspoon black peppercorns, cracked**

⅛   **teaspoon salt**

1   **teaspoon olive oil**

2   **tablespoons minced shallot**

▲ 2   **tablespoons reduced-sodium beef broth**

2   **tablespoons port wine**

1   **teaspoon minced fresh thyme**

½   **teaspoon Worcestershire sauce**

1   Sprinkle steak with peppercorns and salt. Heat ½ teaspoon oil in small skillet over medium-high heat. Add steak and cook, turning once, until instant-read thermometer inserted into side of steak registers 145°F for medium-rare, 6–8 minutes. Transfer to plate and keep warm.

2   Reduce heat to medium. Add remaining ½ teaspoon oil to same skillet. Add shallot and cook, stirring often, until softened, about 2 minutes. Add broth, wine, thyme, and Worcestershire sauce. Bring to boil and cook, stirring often, until slightly thickened, about 2 minutes. Serve steak with sauce.

PER SERVING (1 steak and 2 ½ tablespoons sauce): 273 Cal, 12 g Total Fat, 3 g Sat Fat, 0 g Trans Fat, 67 mg Chol, 419 mg Sod, 8 g Carb, 3 g Sugar, 0 g Fib, 26 g Prot, 33 mg Calc.

FOR YOUR INFO

To crack the peppercorns, use a mortar and pestle, or put them in a small zip-close plastic bag and crack them using a kitchen mallet or heavy skillet.

PUB-STYLE STEAK

SERVES 1

- ▲ 1 (¼-pound) lean filet mignon steak, trimmed
- ⅛ teaspoon salt
- ⅛ teaspoon black pepper
- ¾ teaspoon olive oil
- 1 small shallot, thinly sliced
- 1 small garlic clove, thinly sliced
- ½ teaspoon chopped fresh thyme
- ½ teaspoon tomato paste
- ⅓ cup stout beer
- ▲ ¼ cup reduced-sodium beef or chicken broth
- ½ teaspoon Worcestershire sauce
- ½ teaspoon butter

1 Sprinkle steak with salt and pepper. Heat ½ teaspoon oil in small skillet over medium high-heat. Add steak and cook, turning once, until instant-read thermometer inserted into side of steak registers 145°F for medium-rare, 6–8 minutes. Transfer to plate and keep warm.

2 Reduce heat to medium-low. Add remaining ¼ teaspoon oil to same skillet. Add shallot, garlic, and thyme. Cook, stirring often, until shallot is softened, about 1 minute. Add tomato paste and cook, stirring constantly, 1 minute. Add stout; bring to boil. Cook, stirring often, until almost all liquid evaporates, about 2 minutes. Add broth and Worcestershire sauce; cook, stirring constantly, until sauce thickens slightly, about 1 minute. Remove from heat; stir in butter. Pour sauce over steak.

PER SERVING (1 steak and ¼ cup sauce): 276 Cal, 13 g Total Fat, 4 g Sat Fat, 0 g Trans Fat, 72 mg Chol, 435 mg Sod, 9 g Carb, 1 g Sugar, 0 g Fib, 27 g Prot, 35 mg Calc.

FOR YOUR INFO

Chill the beer before making this dish and enjoy the remaining beer with your meal. Eight ounces of stout beer will add **4 PointsPlus** value.

STEAK WITH SHALLOT–BLUE CHEESE SAUCE

SERVES 1   UNDER 20 MINUTES

▲ 1   (¼-pound) lean filet mignon steak, trimmed

2   pinches salt

2   pinches black pepper

½   teaspoon olive oil

2   small shallots, sliced

1   small garlic clove, minced

2   tablespoons Madeira wine

▲ ¼   cup reduced-sodium chicken broth

1   tablespoon crumbled blue cheese

1 Sprinkle steak with pinch of salt and pinch of pepper. Heat oil in medium skillet over medium-high heat. Add steak and cook, turning once, until instant-read thermometer inserted into side of steak registers 145°F for medium-rare, 6–8 minutes. Transfer to plate and cover to keep warm.

2 Spray skillet with nonstick spray and set over medium heat. Add shallots, garlic, and pinch of salt and pinch of pepper to skillet. Cook, stirring frequently, until shallots begin to soften, 3 minutes. Add wine, scraping up any browned bits from bottom of skillet. Cook until liquid evaporates and shallots are tender, 3–4 minutes longer. Add broth and cook until almost evaporated, 2 minutes.

3 Remove from heat and add cheese. Stir until melted. Spoon sauce over steak.

PER SERVING (1 steak and about ⅓ cup sauce): 241 Cal, 12 g Total Fat, 5 g Sat Fat, 0 g Trans Fat, 78 mg Chol, 574 mg Sod, 5 g Carb, 4 g Sugar, 0 g Fib, 27 g Prot, 64 mg Calc.

6 PointsPlus® value

GRILLED SIRLOIN WITH CREAMY MUSHROOM SAUCE

SERVES 1   UNDER 20 MINUTES

- ▲ 1 **(¼-pound) piece lean boneless sirloin steak, trimmed**
- ¼ **teaspoon black pepper**
- ⅛ **teaspoon salt**
- ½ **teaspoon olive oil**
- ▲ 3 **ounces thinly sliced cremini mushrooms**
- ▲ 1½ **tablespoons reduced-sodium beef broth**
- 1 **tablespoons light garlic and herb cheese spread**

1 Sprinkle steak with ⅛ teaspoon pepper and salt. Spray ridged cast-iron grill pan with nonstick spray; set over medium-high heat. Add steak and grill, turning once, until instant-read thermometer inserted into side of steak registers 145°F for medium-rare, 6–8 minutes. Transfer steak to plate.

2 Meanwhile, to make sauce, heat oil in small nonstick skillet over medium heat. Add mushrooms and remaining ⅛ teaspoon pepper; cook, stirring often, until softened, 3 minutes. Add broth and bring to boil. Remove from heat. Add cheese and stir until melted. Serve steak with mushroom sauce.

PER SERVING (1 steak and ½ cup sauce): 234 Cal, 10 g Total Fat, 4 g Sat Fat, 0 g Trans Fat, 59 mg Chol, 437 mg Sod, 5 g Carb, 3 g Sugar, 1 g Fib, 30 g Prot, 86 mg Calc.

STAY ON TRACK Whole wheat angel hair pasta is perfect along with the saucy mushrooms in this dish (½ cup cooked whole wheat angel hair pasta will increase the *PointsPlus* value by *2*).

Portobello mushrooms make a great single-serve vegetable.
GRILLED BALSAMIC STEAK WITH MUSHROOM AND ASPARAGUS

GRILLED BALSAMIC STEAK WITH MUSHROOM AND ASPARAGUS

SERVES 1   UNDER 20 MINUTES

▲ 1   **(¼-pound) piece lean boneless sirloin steak, trimmed**

¼   **teaspoon salt**

¼   **teaspoon black pepper**

2   **teaspoons balsamic vinegar**

1   **teaspoon olive oil**

▲ 8   **fresh asparagus spears, trimmed and cut crosswise in half**

▲ 1   **portobello mushroom, stem removed**

2   **teaspoons toasted pine nuts**

2   **teaspoons chopped fresh parsley**

1 Sprinkle steak with ⅛ teaspoon salt and ⅛ teaspoon pepper; brush both sides with 1 teaspoon vinegar. Stir together oil, remaining 1 teaspoon vinegar, remaining ⅛ teaspoon salt, and remaining ⅛ teaspoon pepper in medium bowl. Add asparagus and mushroom; turn to coat.

2 Spray ridged cast-iron grill pan with nonstick spray; set over medium-high heat. Add steak and vegetables. Cook, turning once, until vegetables are crisp-tender and instant-read thermometer inserted into side of steak registers 145°F for medium-rare, 6–8 minutes. Transfer steak and vegetables to plate; sprinkle with pine nuts and parsley.

PER SERVING (1 steak, 1 mushroom, about 1 cup asparagus, and 2 teaspoons pine nuts): 299 Cal, 14 g Total Fat, 3 g Sat Fat, 0 g Trans Fat, 49 mg Chol, 645 mg Sod, 14 g Carb, 7 g Sugar, 5 g Fib, 32 g Prot, 66 mg Calc.

STAY ON TRACK   Serve the steak and vegetables with a side dish of white and wild rice blend (½ cup cooked white and wild rice blend will increase the *PointsPlus* value by **2**).

ASIAN BEEF QUESADILLA

SERVES 1   UNDER 20 MINUTES

¼   teaspoon hot Asian
sesame oil

▲ ¼   pound ground lean
beef (7% fat or less)

▲ 1   scallion, finely
chopped

▲ 1   canned water
chestnut, finely
chopped or 2
tablespoons finely
chopped celery

1   teaspoon hoisin
sauce

½   teaspoon reduced-
sodium soy sauce

¼   teaspoon grated
peeled fresh ginger

2   (6-inch) fat-free
whole wheat tortillas

2   tablespoons
shredded low-fat
Monterey Jack
cheese

1 To make filling, heat oil in medium nonstick skillet over medium heat. Add beef and cook, breaking beef apart with wooden spoon, until browned, about 4 minutes. Add scallion, water chestnut, hoisin sauce, soy sauce, and ginger. Cook, stirring occasionally, 1 minute. Transfer to small bowl.

2 Wipe out skillet. Place 1 tortilla in skillet. Sprinkle with 1 tablespoon Monterey Jack. Top with beef mixture, then sprinkle with remaining 1 tablespoon cheese. Top with remaining tortilla. Cook over medium heat, turning once, until cheese is melted and quesadilla is lightly browned, about 4 minutes. Cut quesadilla into quarters.

PER SERVING (1 quesadilla): 449 Cal, 11 g Total Fat, 5 g Sat Fat, 0 g Trans Fat, 76 mg Chol, 985 mg Sod, 51 g Carb, 2 g Sugar, 4 g Fib, 35 g Prot, 277 mg Calc.

TURKISH MEATBALL KEBABS WITH YOGURT-POMEGRANATE SAUCE

SERVES 1

▲ ¼ cup plain fat-free Greek yogurt

1 tablespoon chopped fresh mint

½ teaspoon pomegranate molasses

¼ teaspoon salt

▲ 6 ounces ground lean beef (7% fat or less)

1 tablespoon crumbled feta cheese

1½ teaspoons plain dried bread crumbs

1 garlic clove, minced

½ teaspoon ground cumin

Pinch cayenne

1 Combine yogurt, mint, molasses, and ⅛ teaspoon salt in small bowl. Set aside.

2 To make meatballs, stir together beef, feta, bread crumbs, garlic, cumin, remaining ⅛ teaspoon salt, and cayenne in medium bowl just until well combined. With damp hands, shape mixture into 6 (1½-inch) meatballs.

3 Thread meatballs onto 2 (6-inch) inch skewers. Spray ridged cast-iron grill pan with nonstick spray and set over medium-high heat. Add kebabs and cook, turning occasionally, until browned and cooked through, 10–12 minutes. Serve kebabs with sauce.

PER SERVING (2 kebabs and ¼ cup sauce): 312 Cal, 11 g Total Fat, 5 g Sat Fat, 0 g Trans Fat, 111 mg Chol, 837 mg Sod, 9 g Carb, 5 g Sugar, 1 g Fib, 41 g Prot, 124 mg Calc.

7 PointsPlus value

DOUBLE FENNEL PORK CHOP

SERVES 1

▲ 1 (¼-pound) lean center-cut boneless pork loin chop, trimmed

½ teaspoon fennel seeds, crushed

⅛ teaspoon black pepper

2 pinches salt

1 teaspoon olive oil

▲ ½ small fennel bulb, thinly sliced (fronds reserved)

▲ ½ small red onion, thinly sliced

▲ ½ cubanelle or banana pepper, thinly sliced

3 large green olives, pitted and sliced

1 Sprinkle pork with fennel seeds, black pepper, and 1 pinch salt. Heat ½ teaspoon oil in medium skillet over medium-high heat. Add pork and cook, turning once, until instant-read thermometer inserted into side of chop registers 145°F, about 6 minutes. Transfer to plate and keep warm.

2 Reduce heat to medium. Add remaining ½ teaspoon oil to same skillet. Add fennel bulb, onion, cubanelle pepper, olives, and remaining pinch of salt. Cover and cook, stirring occasionally, until vegetables are lightly browned and tender, 6–7 minutes. Chop enough reserved fennel fronds to equal 1 tablespoon. Stir in fennel fronds. Serve pork chop with fennel mixture.

PER SERVING (1 pork chop and 1¾ cups vegetables): 255 Cal, 12 g Total Fat, 3 g Sat Fat, 0 g Trans Fat, 66 mg Chol, 527 mg Sod, 14 g Carb, 2 g Sugar, 6 g Fib, 24 g Prot, 104 mg Calc.

STAY ON TRACK

Wild rice makes a delicious side dish to accompany the pork chop (½ cup cooked wild rice will increase the *PointsPlus* value by *2*).

PORK CHOP WITH DATES AND PROSCIUTTO

SERVES 1

- ▲ **1** **(¼-pound) lean center-cut boneless pork loin chop, trimmed**
- **2** **pitted dates**
- **⅛** **teaspoon coarsely ground black pepper**
- **1** **thin slice prosciutto (about 1 ounce)**
- **1** **tablespoon balsamic vinegar**

1 Preheat oven to 375°F.

2 Make pocket in side of pork chop by inserting sharp paring knife into thickest part and gently cutting back and forth until large, deep cavity is formed. Fill pocket with dates. Sprinkle chop with pepper and wrap with prosciutto.

3 Spray medium ovenproof skillet with nonstick spray and set over medium-high heat. Add pork chop and cook, turning once, until browned, about 4 minutes. Brush with vinegar.

4 Transfer to oven and bake until instant-read thermometer inserted into side of chop registers 145°F, about 8 minutes.

PER SERVING (1 stuffed pork chop): 262 Cal, 9 g Total Fat, 3 g Sat Fat, 0 g Trans Fat, 89 mg Chol, 807 mg Sod, 16 g Carb, 13 g Sugar, 1 g Fib, 30 g Prot, 31 mg Calc.

STAY ON TRACK A baked sweet potato makes an easy accompaniment for the pork chop (one 5-ounce sweet potato will increase the *PointsPlus* value by **3**).

PAPRIKA PORK WITH GRAPEFRUIT

SERVES 1   UNDER 20 MINUTES

▲ **1 (5-ounce) lean center-cut bone-in pork loin chop, trimmed**

  ¼ teaspoon smoked paprika

  ¼ teaspoon ground coriander

  ¼ teaspoon salt

  ¼ teaspoon black pepper

▲ **1 small grapefruit**

▲ **1 scallion, thinly sliced**

  ½ teaspoon extra-virgin olive oil

1 Sprinkle pork chop with paprika, coriander, ⅛ teaspoon salt, and ⅛ teaspoon pepper. Spray ridged cast-iron grill pan with nonstick spray and set over medium-high heat. Add pork chop and grill, turning once, until instant-read thermometer inserted into side of chop registers 145°F, about 6 minutes.

2 Meanwhile, with small knife, cut away peel and white pith from grapefruit. Working over small bowl, cut between membranes to release segments. Squeeze juice from membranes. Add scallion, oil, remaining ⅛ teaspoon salt, and remaining ⅛ teaspoon pepper to bowl; stir to combine. Serve pork chop with grapefruit mixture.

PER SERVING (1 pork chop and generous ½ cup grapefruit): 218 Cal, 8 g Total Fat, 2 g Sat Fat, 0 g Trans Fat, 59 mg Chol, 624 mg Sod, 18 g Carb, 14 g Sugar, 3 g Fib, 20 g Prot, 55 mg Calc.

STAY ON TRACK

To make a salad to serve with the pork chop, toss together 1 cup mixed baby salad greens, 1 teaspoon white-wine vinegar, and salt and pepper to taste.

Tart citrus is a flavorful counterpoint to a smoky pork chop.
PAPRIKA PORK WITH GRAPEFRUIT

PORK CHOP WITH PLUM-TARRAGON SAUCE

SERVES 1   UNDER 20 MINUTES

▲ 1   **(5-ounce) lean center-cut bone-in loin pork chop, trimmed**

¼   **teaspoon salt**

¼   **teaspoon black pepper**

1   **teaspoon olive oil**

▲ 1   **small onion, finely chopped**

▲ 1   **plum, pitted and thinly sliced**

▲ ¼   **cup reduced-sodium chicken broth**

1½   **teaspoons white-wine vinegar**

¾   **teaspoon turbinado sugar or brown sugar**

1   **teaspoon chopped fresh tarragon**

1 Sprinkle pork chop with ⅛ teaspoon salt and ⅛ teaspoon pepper. Heat ½ teaspoon oil in medium skillet over medium-high heat. Add pork chop and cook, turning once, until instant-read thermometer inserted into side of chop registers 145°F, about 6 minutes. Transfer pork chop to plate and keep warm.

2 Reduce heat to medium-low. Add remaining ½ teaspoon oil to same skillet. Add onion and cook, stirring constantly, until softened, about 1 minute. Add plum, broth, vinegar, turbinado sugar, remaining ⅛ teaspoon salt, and remaining ⅛ teaspoon pepper; bring to boil. Reduce heat and simmer until plum is softened, about 1 minute.

3 Remove from heat; stir in tarragon. Serve pork chop with plum sauce.

PER SERVING (1 pork chop and 1 cup sauce): 250 Cal,
10 g Total Fat, 2 g Sat Fat, 0 g Trans Fat, 59 mg Chol,
643 mg Sod, 19 g Carb, 13 g Sugar, 2 g Fib, 21 g Prot,
48 mg Calc.

STAY ON TRACK

If you'd like to include more veggies in this dish, baby spinach is a delicious addition. Add 1 cup baby spinach to the sauce during the last minute of cooking time.

GRILLED PORK CHOP
WITH WARM PINEAPPLE SLAW

SERVES 1   UNDER 20 MINUTES

- ▲ 1 **(¼-pound) lean center-cut boneless pork loin chop, trimmed**
- ½ **teaspoon ground cumin**
- ¼ **teaspoon salt**
- ⅛ **teaspoon black pepper**
- ½ **teaspoon canola oil**
- ▲ 1 **scallion, cut into 1-inch pieces**
- **Pinch red pepper flakes**
- ▲ ⅔ **cup shredded green cabbage**
- ▲ ½ **small red bell pepper, thinly sliced**
- ▲ ½ **cup diced fresh pineapple**
- **Grated zest and juice of ¼ lime**

1 Sprinkle pork chop with cumin, ⅛ teaspoon salt, and black pepper. Spray ridged cast-iron grill pan with nonstick spray and set over medium-high heat. Add pork chop and grill, turning once, until instant-read thermometer inserted into side of chop registers 145°F, about 6 minutes. Transfer pork to cutting board and keep warm.

2 Meanwhile, heat oil in medium nonstick skillet over medium heat. Add scallion and red pepper flakes; cook, stirring constantly, until fragrant, about 30 seconds. Add cabbage, bell pepper, and remaining ⅛ teaspoon salt. Cook, stirring often, until vegetables are crisp-tender, about 2 minutes. Add pineapple and cook, stirring often, until heated through, about 1 minute. Stir in lime zest and juice.

3 Thinly slice pork chop and serve with slaw.

PER SERVING (1 pork chop and 1 ½ cups slaw): 241 Cal, 9 g Total Fat, 2 g Sat Fat, 0 g Trans Fat, 66 mg Chol, 641 mg Sod, 19 g Carb, 10 g Sugar, 4 g Fib, 23 g Prot, 78 mg Calc.

Look for tamarind concentrate in specialty food stores.
TAMARIND LAMB KEBABS

TAMARIND LAMB KEBABS

SERVES 1

⅓ cup orange juice

½ teaspoon tamarind concentrate or fresh lemon juice

¼ teaspoon honey

Pinch red pepper flakes

½ teaspoon olive oil

½ teaspoon ground coriander

⅛ teaspoon salt

⅛ teaspoon black pepper

 1 (¼-pound) piece lean boneless leg of lamb, trimmed and cut into 8 pieces

 ½ small zucchini, halved lengthwise then cut crosswise into 8 pieces

1 Combine orange juice, tamarind, honey, and red pepper flakes in small saucepan; bring to boil over high heat. Reduce heat to medium and simmer until mixture is reduced to syrupy glaze, 3–4 minutes. Transfer to small bowl.

2 Stir together oil, coriander, salt, and black pepper in small bowl. Add lamb and toss to coat. Alternately thread lamb and zucchini onto 2 (8-inch) skewers.

3 Spray ridged cast-iron grill pan with nonstick spray and set over medium-high heat. Add kebabs and cook, turning often and basting with half of glaze (scant 1 tablespoon), 8–10 minutes for medium-rare. Serve kebabs with remaining glaze.

PER SERVING (2 kebabs and scant 1 tablespoon glaze): 224 Cal, 8 g Total Fat, 3 g Sat Fat, 0 g Trans Fat, 73 mg Chol, 390 mg Sod, 12 g Carb, 3 g Sugar, 1 g Fib, 25 g Prot, 27 mg Calc.

STAY ON TRACK Add any quick-cooking vegetables you have on hand to the skewers. Try cherry tomatoes, bell peppers, or yellow squash.

CHIPOTLE-ORANGE GRILLED LAMB CHOPS

SERVES 1   UNDER 20 MINUTES

1   **teaspoon minced chipotles en adobo**

1   **teaspoon grated orange zest**

2   **teaspoons orange juice**

¼   **teaspoon ground cumin**

⅛   **teaspoon salt**

▲ 2   **(3-ounce) lean bone-in loin lamb chops, trimmed**

2   **teaspoons minced fresh mint**

1 Stir together chipotles, orange zest and juice, cumin, and salt in small shallow dish. Add chops and turn to coat.

2 Spray ridged cast-iron grill pan with nonstick spray and set over medium-high heat. Add lamb chops and grill, turning once, until instant-read thermometer inserted into sides of chops registers 145°F, about 6 minutes. Transfer chops to plate; sprinkle with mint.

PER SERVING (2 lamb chops): 166 Cal, 7 g Total Fat, 2 g Sat Fat, 0 g Trans Fat, 68 mg Chol, 376 mg Sod, 2 g Carb, 0 g Sugar, 1 g Fib, 22 g Prot, 25 mg Calc.

STAY ON TRACK

To grill a sliced red bell pepper to serve alongside, spray the slices with nonstick spray and grill, turning occasionally, until crisp-tender, 8–10 minutes.

GRILLED LEMONY LAMB BURGER

SERVES 1   UNDER 20 MINUTES

- ¼ **pound ground lean lamb**
- 1 **teaspoon capers, minced**
- ½ **teaspoon whole-grain mustard**
- ½ **teaspoon grated lemon zest**
- ⅛ **teaspoon salt**
- ⅛ **teaspoon black pepper**
- ▲ 1 **plum tomato, halved lengthwise**
- ▲ ¾ **cup arugula**
- 2 **tablespoons fresh mint leaves, torn**

  Lemon wedge

1 Stir together lamb, capers, mustard, and lemon zest in small bowl just until well combined. With damp hands, shape mixture into 1 (¼-inch-thick) patty. Sprinkle with salt and pepper.

2 Spray ridged cast-iron grill pan with nonstick spray and set over medium-high heat. Add patty and tomato, cut side down. Cook, turning once, until instant-read thermometer inserted into side of burger registers 160°F and tomato is evenly charred, about 8 minutes.

3 Combine arugula and mint on plate; top with burger and tomato. Serve with lemon wedge.

PER SERVING (1 burger, 1 tomato, and ¾ cup arugula): 164 Cal, 7 g Total Fat, 2 g Sat Fat, 0 g Trans Fat, 64 mg Chol, 493 mg Sod, 4 g Carb, 2 g Sugar, 1 g Fib, 21 g Prot, 55 mg Calc.

BUFFALO-STYLE GRILLED CHICKEN

SERVES 1 UNDER 20 MINUTES

1 **teaspoon canola oil**

½ **teaspoon smoked paprika**

¼ **teaspoon salt**

⅛ **teaspoon black pepper**

Pinch cayenne

▲ 1 **(¼-pound) skinless boneless chicken breast**

2 **tablespoons reduced-calorie blue cheese dressing**

▲ 2 **radishes**

1 Stir together oil, paprika, salt, pepper, and cayenne in small shallow dish. Add chicken and turn to coat.

2 Spray ridged cast-iron grill pan with nonstick spray and set over medium-high heat. Add chicken and grill, turning once, until browned and cooked through, about 8 minutes. Transfer to plate; drizzle with dressing. Serve with radishes.

PER SERVING (1 chicken breast, 2 tablespoons dressing, and 2 radishes): 220 Cal, 9 g Total Fat, 1 g Sat Fat, 0 g Trans Fat, 63 mg Chol, 965 mg Sod, 10 g Carb, 4 g Sugar, 2 g Fib, 23 g Prot, 35 mg Calc.

STAY ON TRACK

Have this spicy chicken with a cool pea shoot salad: Toss together 1 cup pea shoots, 1 teaspoon lemon juice, and salt and pepper to taste.

All the flavors of your favorite wings—made healthier.
BUFFALO-STYLE GRILLED CHICKEN

SAUTÉED CHICKEN WITH SCALLION-BACON VINAIGRETTE

SERVES 1   UNDER 20 MINUTES

---

1   **slice bacon, cut into ½-inch pieces**

▲ 1   **(¼-pound) skinless boneless chicken breast**

¼   **teaspoon paprika**

⅛   **teaspoon black pepper**

Pinch salt

▲ 2   **medium scallions, thinly sliced**

▲ 2   **tablespoons reduced-sodium chicken broth**

2   **teaspoons white balsamic vinegar**

1 Place bacon in medium nonstick skillet; set over medium heat. Cook, stirring occasionally, until crisp, 2–3 minutes. With slotted spoon, transfer bacon to plate lined with paper towels and drain. Pour off and discard all but ½ teaspoon of bacon drippings.

2 Sprinkle chicken with paprika, pepper, and salt. Add chicken to same skillet and cook, turning once, until cooked through, about 8 minutes. Transfer chicken to plate.

3 To make vinaigrette, add scallions to same skillet; cook, stirring constantly until softened, 1 minute. Add broth and vinegar; bring to boil. Cook, stirring constantly, until liquid is reduced by half, about 1 minute. Stir in bacon. Spoon vinaigrette over chicken.

PER SERVING (1 chicken breast and 3 tablespoons vinaigrette): 257 Cal, 6 g Total Fat, 2 g Sat Fat, 0 g Trans Fat, 110 mg Chol, 609 mg Sod, 5 g Carb, 2 g Sugar, 1 g Fib, 42 g Prot, 47 mg Calc.

6 PointsPlus value

FOR YOUR INFO

White balsamic vinegar is a lighter, sweeter cousin of the more common dark balsamic vinegar. If you don't have any on hand, use white wine vinegar in this recipe.

SPANISH CHICKEN WITH CHORIZO RICE

SERVES 1   UNDER 20 MINUTES

- ▲ 1   **(¼-pound) skinless boneless chicken breast**
- ⅛   **teaspoon salt**
- ⅛   **teaspoon black pepper**
- 1   **teaspoon olive oil**
- ▲ ½   **small onion, finely chopped**
- 1   **ounce soy chorizo, crumbled**
- ▲ ½   **cup cooked brown rice**
- ▲ ¼   **cup thawed frozen peas**
- ▲ 2   **tablespoons chopped roasted red peppers (not oil-packed)**
- 1   **small garlic clove, minced**

1 Sprinkle chicken with salt and black pepper. Heat ½ teaspoon oil in medium nonstick skillet over medium heat. Add chicken and cook, turning once, until browned and cooked through, about 8 minutes. Transfer to plate and keep warm.

2 Add remaining ½ teaspoon oil to same skillet. Add onion and chorizo; cook, stirring occasionally, until onion is tender, 3–4 minutes. Add rice, peas, roasted peppers, and garlic. Cook, stirring occasionally, until heated through, about 1 minute. Serve chicken with rice.

PER SERVING (1 chicken breast and 1 cup rice): 393 Cal, 13 g Total Fat, 2 g Sat Fat, 0 g Trans Fat, 63 mg Chol, 718 mg Sod, 37 g Carb, 5 g Sugar, 7 g Fib, 31 g Prot, 87 mg Calc.

10 PointsPlus® value

STAY ON TRACK

Serve this dish with a refreshing orange and fennel salad: Toss together ½ cup orange segments, ½ cup thinly sliced fresh fennel, and salt and black pepper to taste.

CHICKEN AND VEGETABLES WITH CREAMY PESTO SAUCE

SERVES 1   UNDER 20 MINUTES

1   **slice bacon, coarsely chopped**

▲ 1   **(¼-pound) skinless boneless chicken breast, cut crosswise into thirds**

⅛   **teaspoon salt**

⅛   **teaspoon black pepper**

▲ ½   **small yellow bell pepper, thinly sliced**

▲ ½   **small onion, thinly sliced**

▲ 1½   **cups lightly packed baby spinach**

▲ ½   **cup grape tomatoes, halved**

▲ 2   **tablespoons fat-free half-and-half**

1½   **teaspoons pesto**

1 Place bacon in medium nonstick skillet; set over medium heat. Cook, stirring occasionally, until crisp, 2–3 minutes. With slotted spoon, transfer bacon to plate lined with paper towels and drain. Pour off and discard all but ½ teaspoon of bacon drippings.

2 Sprinkle chicken with salt and black pepper. Add chicken, bell pepper, and onion to skillet. Cook, stirring often, until chicken is browned and cooked through, about 8 minutes.

3 Add spinach, tomatoes, half-and-half, and pesto to skillet. Cook, stirring often, until spinach wilts and sauce is slightly thickened, 1–2 minutes. Transfer to plate; sprinkle with bacon.

PER SERVING (1 chicken breast and 1 cup vegetables and sauce): 291 Cal, 10 g Total Fat, 3 g Sat Fat, 0 g Trans Fat, 74 mg Chol, 688 mg Sod, 20 g Carb, 8 g Sugar, 4 g Fib, 31 g Prot, 123 mg Calc.

STAY ON TRACK

Serve this saucy dish over a bed of whole wheat fettuccine (½ cup cooked whole wheat fettuccine will increase the **PointsPlus** value by **2**).

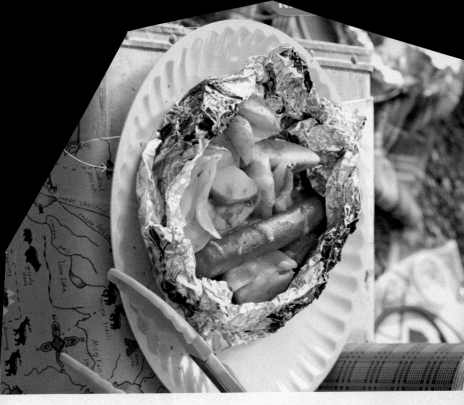

For these nifty foil packs, small hands make quick work of topping potato wedges with a hot dog, onions and cheese.
—KELLY WESTPHAL WIND LAKE, WI

START TO FINISH: 20 MIN. • **MAKES:** 4 SERVINGS

- 1 pkg. (20 oz.) refrigerated red potato wedges
- 4 hot dogs
- 1 small onion, cut into wedges
- ¼ cup shredded cheddar cheese
- ½ cup barbecue sauce

1. Divide potato wedges among four pieces of heavy-duty foil (about 18 in. square). Top each with a hot dog, onion wedges and cheese. Drizzle with barbecue sauce. Fold foil around mixture, sealing tightly.

2. Grill, covered, over medium heat 10-15 minutes or until heated through. Open foil carefully to allow steam to escape.

PER SERVING 293 cal., 16 g fat (7 g sat. fat), 33 mg chol., 1,227 mg sodium, 25 g carb., 4 g fiber, 11 g pro.

The first s'mores recipe appeared in the 1927 Girl Scout handbook. Swap a Thin Mint or a Tagalong for the Oreo if you like!

CHICKEN WITH OKRA RELISH

SERVES 1

- ¾ teaspoon olive oil
- ▲ 3 large fresh okra pods, cut crosswise into thirds
- ½ shallot, thinly sliced
- ▲ ¼ jalapeño pepper, thinly sliced
- ▲ 4 cherry tomatoes, halved
- 1 small garlic clove, thinly sliced
- ¼ teaspoon salt
- 1½ teaspoons sherry vinegar
- 1 tablespoon toasted walnuts, chopped
- ½ teaspoon butter
- ▲ 1 (¼-pound) skinless boneless chicken breast
- ⅛ teaspoon black pepper

1 To make relish, heat ½ teaspoon oil in nonstick skillet over medium heat. Add okra and cook, stirring often, until softened, about 2 minutes. Add shallot and jalapeño; reduce heat and cover. Cook, stirring often, until shallot is softened, about 1 minute. Add tomatoes, garlic, and ⅛ teaspoon salt. Cover and cook, stirring occasionally, until tomatoes soften, about 2 minutes. Stir in vinegar. Transfer mixture to small bowl. Stir in walnuts and butter.

2 Meanwhile, sprinkle chicken with remaining ⅛ teaspoon salt and black pepper.

3 Heat remaining ¼ teaspoon oil in small skillet over medium-high heat. Add chicken and cook, turning once, until cooked through, about 8 minutes. Transfer chicken to plate; top with relish.

PER SERVING (1 chicken breast and scant 1 cup relish): 249 Cal, 13 g Total Fat, 3 g Sat Fat, 0 g Trans Fat, 68 mg Chol, 657 mg Sod, 8 g Carb, 3 g Sugar, 2 g Fib, 26 g Prot, 61 mg Calc.

HAM AND SWISS–STUFFED CHICKEN WITH GARLIC SPINACH

SERVES 1   UNDER 20 MINUTES

▲ 1   **(3-ounce) thin-sliced chicken breast cutlet**

   Pinch black pepper

½   **teaspoon Dijon mustard**

▲ 1   **(1-ounce) slice reduced-sodium lean ham**

1   **tablespoon shredded Swiss cheese**

½   **teaspoon canola oil**

▲ ¼   **cup reduced-sodium chicken broth**

2   **tablespoons dry white wine**

1   **small garlic clove, minced**

▲ 2   **cups lightly packed baby spinach**

   Pinch salt

1 Sprinkle chicken with pepper. Brush one side of chicken with mustard. Top with ham and cheese. Roll cutlet up and secure with wooden toothpicks.

2 Heat oil in medium nonstick skillet over medium heat. Add chicken and cook, turning occasionally, until lightly browned, 5 minutes. Add broth and wine and bring to boil. Cover, reduce heat and simmer until chicken is cooked through, 6–8 minutes. Transfer to plate and cover to keep warm.

3 Add garlic to skillet and cook, stirring constantly, until fragrant, 1 minute. Add spinach and pinch of salt to skillet and cook, stirring frequently, until spinach is wilted, about 1 minute. Remove toothpicks from chicken and serve chicken with spinach.

PER SERVING (1 stuffed chicken cutlet and about ½ cup spinach): 231 Cal, 9 g Total Fat, 3 g Sat Fat, 0 g Trans Fat, 74 mg Chol, 727 mg Sod, 5 g Carb, 1 Sugar, 1 g Fib, 30 g Prot, 139 mg Calc.

6 PointsPlus® value

SAUTÉED CHICKEN WITH OLIVE-CAPER TOMATOES

SERVES 1 UNDER 20 MINUTES

- ▲ 1 **(¼-pound) skinless boneless chicken breast**
- ⅛ **teaspoon salt**
- ⅛ **teaspoon black pepper**
- 1 **teaspoon olive oil**
- ▲ 1 **small onion, finely chopped**
- 1 **small garlic clove, minced**
- ⅛ **teaspoon anchovy paste**
- ▲ 1½ **cups cherry or grape tomatoes, halved**
- 2 **kalamata olives, pitted and chopped**
- 1½ **teaspoons chopped fresh parsley**
- 1 **teaspoon capers, minced**

1 Sprinkle chicken with salt and pepper. Heat ½ teaspoon oil in medium skillet over medium-high heat. Add chicken and cook, turning once, until cooked through, about 8 minutes. Transfer to plate and keep warm.

2 Reduce heat to medium. Add remaining ½ teaspoon oil to same skillet. Add onion and cook, stirring occasionally, until softened, 2–3 minutes. Add garlic and anchovy paste; cook, stirring constantly, until fragrant, about 30 seconds. Add tomatoes and cook, stirring occasionally, until softened, 3–4 minutes. Stir in olives, parsley, and capers. Serve chicken with tomatoes.

PER SERVING (1 chicken cutlet and 1 ⅓ cups tomatoes): 259 Cal, 10 g Total Fat, 2 g Sat Fat, 0 g Trans Fat, 66 mg Chol, 630 mg Sod, 17 g Carb, 9 g Sugar, 4 g Fib, 26 g Prot, 63 mg Calc.

FOR YOUR INFO

Anchovy paste, sold in tubes, is a convenient and versatile ingredient to keep on hand. You can squeeze out a tiny bit to add to sauces, salad dressings, and soups.

GRILLED LEMON CHICKEN WITH SPRING PEA SAUTÉ

SERVES 1   UNDER 20 MINUTES

½   **small lemon**

¾   **teaspoon horseradish mustard or Dijon mustard**

1   **small garlic clove, minced**

▲ 1   **(¼-pound) skinless boneless chicken breast**

½   **teaspoon olive oil**

▲ ¼   **pound fresh snow peas, trimmed**

▲ ⅓   **cup thawed frozen green peas**

⅛   **teaspoon salt**

⅛   **teaspoon black pepper**

1½   **teaspoons snipped fresh chives**

1 Grate zest from lemon. Stir together lemon zest, mustard, and garlic in small shallow dish. Add chicken and turn to coat. Spray ridged cast-iron grill pan with nonstick spray and set over medium heat. Add chicken and lemon, cut side down. Cook, turning once, until chicken is cooked through and lemon is well charred, about 8 minutes.

2 Meanwhile, heat oil in medium nonstick skillet over medium heat. Add snow peas, green peas, salt, and pepper. Cook, stirring often, until peas are crisp-tender, about 2 minutes.

3 Cut lemon in half. Transfer peas to plate and top with chicken. Sprinkle chicken with chives and serve with lemon.

PER SERVING (1 chicken breast, 1 ⅔ cups peas, and ½ lemon): 248 Cal, 6 g Total Fat, 1 g Sat Fat, 0 g Trans Fat, 63 mg Chol, 420 mg Sod, 22 g Carb, 6 g Sugar, 8 g Fib, 29 g Prot, 120 mg Calc.

Try this fresh, fast, flavorful dish to welcome spring.
GRILLED LEMON CHICKEN WITH SPRING PEA SAUTÉ

CHICKEN AND EGG FRIED RICE

SERVES 1   UNDER 20 MINUTES

½ teaspoon Asian (dark) sesame oil

▲ 1 (3-ounce) thin-sliced chicken breast cutlet, cut into thin strips

▲ 1 scallion, thinly sliced

▲ 1 small celery stalk, thinly sliced

½ teaspoon grated peeled fresh ginger

▲ ½ cup thawed frozen peas

▲ ½ cup cooked brown rice

1 tablespoon reduced-sodium soy sauce

▲ 1 large egg, lightly beaten

2 teaspoons chopped fresh cilantro

1 Heat sesame oil in medium nonstick skillet over medium heat. Add chicken, and cook, stirring often, until chicken is lightly browned, 4 minutes. Add scallion, celery, and ginger. Stir-fry until softened, about 2 minutes. Add peas, rice, and soy sauce. Cook until heated through, about 3 minutes. Transfer mixture to serving bowl and cover to keep warm.

2 Spray same skillet with nonstick spray and set over medium heat. Add egg and cook stirring occasionally, until scrambled and cooked through, 1 minute. Stir egg into rice mixture. Sprinkle with cilantro.

PER SERVING (1¾ cups): 381 Cal, 12 g Total Fat, 3 g Sat Fat, 0 g Trans Fat, 239 mg Chol, 708 mg Sod, 36 g Carb, 5 g Sugar, 6 g Fib, 33 g Prot, 81 mg Calc.

10 PointsPlus® value

CHICKEN-MUSHROOM SOFT TACOS

SERVES 1 UNDER 20 MINUTES

½ teaspoon olive oil

▲ 1 (¼-pound) skinless, boneless chicken breast, cut into thin strips

⅛ teaspoon ground cumin

▲ 4 white mushrooms, sliced

▲ 2 tablespoons minced onion

1 small garlic clove, minced

▲ ⅓ cup fat-free salsa

2 (6-inch) whole wheat tortillas, warmed

2 tablespoons shredded reduced-fat Monterey Jack cheese

1 tablespoon chopped fresh cilantro

1 Heat oil in large nonstick skillet over medium heat. Sprinkle chicken with cumin and add to skillet. Cook, stirring often, until chicken is lightly browned, 4 minutes. Transfer to plate.

2 Spray skillet with nonstick spray and set over medium heat. Add mushrooms, onion, and garlic to skillet and cook, stirring often, until vegetables are tender, 6 minutes. Add chicken and salsa and cook until heated through, about 2 minutes.

3 Spoon chicken mixture into tortillas. Top with Monterey Jack and cilantro.

PER SERVING (2 tacos): 358 Cal, 11 g Total Fat, 4 g Sat Fat, 0 g Trans Fat, 80 mg Chol, 875 mg Sod, 30 g Carb, 5 g Sugar, 5 g Fib, 37 g Prot, 160 mg Calc.

9 PointsPlus® value

HERBED TURKEY CUTLET WITH BRANDIED PEARS

SERVES 1   UNDER 20 MINUTES

▲ 1 (¼-pound) turkey breast cutlet

¼ teaspoon salt

2 pinches black pepper

½ teaspoon olive oil

½ teaspoon butter

1 shallot, finely chopped

▲ ½ Bartlett pear, cored and cut into 6 wedges

1½ teaspoons brandy

▲ 2 tablespoons reduced-sodium chicken broth

▲ 2 tablespoons fat-free half-and-half

2 teaspoons chopped fresh thyme

1 Sprinkle turkey with ⅛ teaspoon salt and 1 pinch pepper. Heat oil in medium skillet over medium-high heat. Add turkey and cook, turning once, until browned and cooked through, 6–8 minutes. Transfer to plate and keep warm.

2 Reduce heat to medium-low. Add butter to same skillet. Add shallot, pear, remaining ⅛ teaspoon salt, and remaining pinch of pepper. Cover and cook, stirring occasionally, until pear and shallot are softened, about 2 minutes. Add brandy; bring to boil. Add broth and half-and-half. Cook, stirring occasionally, until sauce is slightly thickened and pear is tender, 1½–2 minutes. Stir in thyme. Spoon pear mixture over turkey.

PER SERVING (1 turkey cutlet and ¾ cup pear mixture): 275 Cal, 5 g Total Fat, 2 g Sat Fat, 0 g Trans Fat, 50 mg Chol, 734 mg Sod, 23 g Carb, 23 g Sugar, 3 g Fib, 31 g Prot, 69 mg Calc.

TURKEY SCALOPPINI WITH CHERRY TOMATO–SWEET CORN SAUCE

SERVES 1   UNDER 20 MINUTES

▲ 1   **(¼-pound) turkey breast cutlet, pounded to ⅛-inch thickness**

¼   **teaspoon salt**

Pinch black pepper

1   **teaspoon olive oil**

▲ ¼   **cup finely chopped red onion**

1   **small garlic clove, minced**

Pinch red pepper flakes

¼   **cup dry white wine**

▲ 1   **cup cherry tomatoes, halved**

▲ ⅓   **cup fresh or thawed frozen corn kernels**

1   **tablespoon thinly sliced fresh basil**

1 Sprinkle turkey with ⅛ teaspoon salt and black pepper. Heat ½ teaspoon oil in medium skillet over medium-high heat. Add turkey and cook, turning once, until browned and cooked through, 6–8 minutes. Transfer turkey to plate and keep warm.

2 Reduce heat to medium. Add remaining ½ teaspoon oil to same skillet. Add onion and cook, stirring often, until softened, about 1 minute. Add garlic and red pepper flakes; cook, stirring constantly, until fragrant, about 30 seconds. Stir in wine; bring to boil. Reduce heat and simmer until liquid has almost evaporated, 1–1 ½ minutes. Stir in tomatoes and remaining ⅛ teaspoon salt. Cook, stirring often, until tomatoes soften, 1–2 minutes.

3 With back of wooden spoon, lightly crush tomatoes. Stir in corn and cook until heated through, about 1 minute. Remove skillet from heat; stir in basil. Serve turkey with tomato mixture.

PER SERVING (1 turkey cutlet and 1 cup sauce): 301 Cal, 6 g Total Fat, 1 g Sat Fat, 0 g Trans Fat, 45 mg Chol, 699 mg Sod, 22 g Carb, 7 g Sugar, 4 g Fib, 32 g Prot, 36 mg Calc.

FOR YOUR INFO

To pound the turkey cutlet, place it between two sheets of plastic wrap on a cutting board. Using a meat mallet or a small heavy skillet, pound the turkey until it is ⅛-inch thick.

SWEET CHILI–TERIYAKI SALMON WITH SESAME VEGETABLES

SERVES 1   UNDER 20 MINUTES

1	**teaspoon teriyaki sauce**
½	**teaspoon Asian sweet chili sauce**
	Grated zest and juice of ¼ lime
½	**teaspoon canola oil**
1	**(5-ounce) skinless salmon fillet**
¼	**teaspoon Asian (dark) sesame oil**
▲ **2½**	**cups precut fresh vegetables for stir-fry**
2	**tablespoons water**
⅛	**teaspoon salt**
	Lime wedge

1 To make glaze, stir together teriyaki sauce, chili sauce, and lime zest and juice in small bowl.

2 Heat canola oil in small nonstick skillet over medium heat. Add salmon and cook until underside is browned, about 2 minutes. Turn salmon, brush with half of glaze, and cook until bottom is browned, about 2 minutes. Turn salmon again, brush with remaining glaze, and cook until just opaque in center, about 1 minute. Transfer to plate and keep warm.

3 Meanwhile, heat sesame oil in medium nonstick skillet over medium heat. Add vegetables, water, and salt. Cover and cook, stirring occasionally, until vegetables are crisp-tender, about 2 minutes. Serve salmon and vegetables with lime wedge.

PER SERVING (1 salmon fillet and 2 cups vegetables):
406 Cal, 14 g Total Fat, 2 g Sat Fat, 0 g Trans Fat, 90 mg Chol, 671 mg Sod, 30 g Carb, 11 g Sugar, 5 g Fib, 37 g Prot, 72 mg Calc.

FOR YOUR INFO

Look for precut fresh vegetables for stir-fry in the supermarket produce section near the packaged salads. Or, customize your own blend by selecting precut veggies from the salad bar.

POTATO-WRAPPED ROASTED SALMON

SERVES 1

- **1** **(4-ounce) skinless salmon fillet**
- **2** **teaspoons Dijon mustard**
- ▲ **1** **long Yukon Gold potato, peeled**
- **Pinch salt**
- **Pinch black pepper**
- **½** **teaspoon olive oil**
- ▲ **1** **tablespoon reduced-sodium chicken broth**
- **2** **teaspoons white-wine vinegar**
- **1** **teaspoon red currant jelly**

1 Preheat oven to 375°F.

2 Brush salmon with mustard.

3 With vegetable peeler, cut 8–10 lengthwise slices from potato. Reserve remaining potato for another use. Place potato slices on work surface, overlapping long sides. Place salmon in center of potatoes, perpendicular to potato slices. Fold potato slices over salmon, pressing to adhere. Sprinkle with salt and pepper.

4 Heat oil in small ovenproof nonstick skillet over medium heat. Add salmon, seam side down, and cook until bottom is browned, about 4 minutes. Carefully turn over salmon. Transfer skillet to oven. Bake until bottom is lightly browned and salmon is just opaque in center, about 10 minutes.

5 Transfer salmon to plate. Set same skillet over medium heat; add broth, vinegar, and jelly. Cook, stirring constantly, until mixture comes to boil, about 1 minute. Pour sauce over salmon.

PER SERVING (1 salmon fillet and 1 tablespoon sauce): 258 Cal, 14 g Total Fat, 3 g Sat Fat, 0 g Trans Fat, 47 mg Chol, 618 mg Sod, 14 g Carb, 4 g Sugar, 1 g Fib, 18 g Prot, 12 mg Calc.

STAY ON TRACK Steamed spinach makes a colorful and delicious side dish for the salmon.

BASIL-CRUSTED SALMON
WITH CUCUMBER-TOMATO SALSA

SERVES 1   UNDER 20 MINUTES

▲ 1 **Kirby cucumber, peeled and chopped**

▲ 1 **plum tomato, chopped**

▲ ½ **medium jalapeño pepper, seeded and minced**

3 **tablespoons chopped fresh basil**

▲ 2 **tablespoons finely chopped red onion**

1 **tablespoon fresh lime juice**

2 **pinches salt**

1 **(¼-pound) salmon fillet**

Pinch black pepper

1 To make salsa, stir together cucumber, tomato, jalapeño, 2 tablespoons basil, onion, lime juice, and pinch of salt in small bowl.

2 Spray medium skillet with nonstick spray and set over medium heat. Sprinkle salmon with remaining pinch of salt and pepper. Sprinkle with remaining 1 tablespoon basil. Place salmon in skillet and cook until opaque in center, 4–5 minutes on each side. Serve salmon with salsa.

PER SERVING (1 salmon fillet and 1 cup salsa): 214 Cal, 12 g Total Fat, 3 g Sat Fat, 0 g Trans Fat, 47 mg Chol, 347 mg Sod, 8 g Carb, 4 g Sugar, 2 g Fib, 19 g Prot, 47 mg Calc.

PORCINI-CRUSTED COD WITH THYME SAUCE

SERVES 1   UNDER 20 MINUTES

▲ **1½ tablespoons crumbled dried porcini mushrooms**

▲ **1   (5-ounce) cod fillet**

⅛   teaspoon salt

⅛   teaspoon black pepper

1   teaspoon olive oil

1   tablespoon dry white wine

▲ **1   tablespoon reduced-sodium chicken broth**

½   teaspoon minced fresh thyme

1 Place mushrooms in spice grinder and pulse until finely ground. Sprinkle cod with mushrooms, salt, and pepper.

2 Heat oil in small skillet over medium-high heat. Add cod and cook, turning once, just until opaque in center, about 6 minutes. Transfer cod to plate.

3 Add wine, broth, and thyme to skillet; bring to boil, stirring constantly. Pour sauce over fish.

PER SERVING (1 cod fillet and 1 tablespoon sauce):
206 Cal, 6 g Total Fat, 1 g Sat Fat, 0 g Trans Fat, 54 mg Chol, 377 mg Sod, 7 g Carb, 0 g Sugar, 2 g Fib, 27 g Prot, 21 mg Calc.

5 PointsPlus® value

FOR YOUR INFO

The dried mushrooms add an earthy note to this dish, but if you wish, you can omit them and the fish will still be delicious.

PAN-SEARED COD WITH ASIAN CUCUMBER SALAD

SERVES 1   UNDER 20 MINUTES

▲ 1   **small red onion, thinly sliced**

▲ ¼   **English (seedless) cucumber, thinly sliced**

¼   **teaspoon salt**

▲ 1   **(5-ounce) cod fillet**

⅛   **teaspoon black pepper**

1   **teaspoon canola oil**

1   **teaspoon rice vinegar**

1   **teaspoon finely chopped pickled ginger**

1 To make salad, place onion in colander and rinse under cold running water; drain. Transfer to medium bowl. Add cucumber and ⅛ teaspoon salt; toss to combine. Let stand, stirring occasionally, until cucumber and onion soften, about 10 minutes.

2 Meanwhile, sprinkle cod with remaining ⅛ teaspoon salt and pepper. Heat ½ teaspoon oil in small nonstick skillet over medium heat. Add cod and cook, turning once, until just opaque in center, about 6 minutes.

3 Stir remaining ½ teaspoon oil, vinegar, and ginger into salad. Serve cod with salad.

PER SERVING (1 cod fillet and about 1 cup salad): 187 Cal, 6 g Total Fat, 1 g Sat Fat, 0 g Trans Fat, 54 mg Chol, 694 mg Sod, 10 g Carb, 4 g Sugar, 2 g Fib, 24 g Prot, 49 mg Calc.

5 PointsPlus® value

This cucumber salad goes great with salmon or shrimp too.
PAN-SEARED COD WITH ASIAN CUCUMBER SALAD

STEAMED STRIPED BASS WITH GINGERY MUSHROOMS

SERVES 1   UNDER 20 MINUTES

▲ 1   **cup thinly sliced mixed wild mushrooms (2 ounces)**

1   **teaspoon chopped peeled fresh ginger**

▲ 1   **scallion, sliced**

▲ 1   **(6-ounce) striped bass fillet**

1½   **teaspoons reduced-sodium soy sauce**

1   **slice Canadian bacon, finely diced**

1 Line steamer basket with foil. Place half of mushrooms, half of ginger, and half of scallion on foil; place fish on top of mushroom mixture. Top with remaining mushrooms, ginger, and scallion. Drizzle with soy sauce and sprinkle with Canadian bacon.

2 Set steamer basket in large deep skillet over 1 inch of boiling water. Cover tightly and steam until fish is just opaque in center and mushrooms are tender, 8–10 minutes.

PER SERVING (1 fillet and about ½ cup mushrooms): 242 Cal, 6 g Total Fat, 2 g Sat Fat, 0 g Trans Fat, 154 mg Chol, 757 mg Sod, 5 g Carb, 2 g Sugar, 1 g Fib, 39 g Prot, 54 mg Calc.

FOR YOUR INFO

You can use any mild fish fillet for this recipe: Try catfish, sole, or cod.

GRILLED TUNA WITH WARM RADICCHIO SALAD

SERVES 1 UNDER 20 MINUTES

1 teaspoon extra-virgin olive oil

½ teaspoon balsamic vinegar

¼ teaspoon salt

¼ teaspoon black pepper

¼ cup fresh flat-leaf parsley leaves

2 teaspoons golden raisins

2 teaspoons toasted sliced almonds

▲ 1 small radicchio di Treviso, cut crosswise in half and leaves separated

▲ 1 small Belgian endive, cut crosswise in half and leaves separated

▲ 1 (5-ounce) tuna steak

1 To make dressing, whisk together oil, vinegar, ⅛ teaspoon salt and ⅛ teaspoon pepper in medium bowl. Stir in parsley, raisins, and almonds.

2 Spray ridged cast-iron grill pan with nonstick spray and set over medium-high heat. Add radicchio and Belgian endive, in batches if necessary, and cook, turning once, until edges of leaves brown, about 2 minutes. Transfer to bowl with dressing; toss to coat.

3 Sprinkle tuna with remaining ⅛ teaspoon salt and remaining ⅛ teaspoon pepper. Spray same grill pan with nonstick spray. Add tuna and cook, turning once, until pink in center, 4–6 minutes. Serve tuna with salad.

PER SERVING (1 tuna steak and 2½ cups salad): 302 Cal, 14 g Total Fat, 3 g Sat Fat, 0 g Trans Fat, 52 mg Chol, 648 mg Sod, 11 g Carb, 4 g Sugar, 4 g Fib, 34 g Prot, 67 mg Calc.

FOR YOUR INFO Radicchio di Treviso has white ribs and narrow pointed leaves that can range from pink to dark red. You can substitute a round radicchio or another head of Belgian endive.

*Cook up this comforting
Tex-Mex favorite in minutes.*
SHRIMP POSOLE

SHRIMP POSOLE

SERVES 1   UNDER 20 MINUTES

1   teaspoon canola oil

▲ 1   small onion, finely chopped

1   clove garlic, finely chopped

¼   teaspoon ground cumin

¼   teaspoon dried oregano

½   cup canned crushed tomatillos

▲ ⅓   cup reduced-sodium chicken broth

▲ ⅓   cup canned hominy, rinsed and drained

▲ 4   jumbo peeled and deveined shrimp (5 ounces)

▲ ⅓   cup fresh or thawed frozen corn kernels

2   teaspoons chopped fresh cilantro

⅛   teaspoon salt

⅛   teaspoon black pepper

1 Heat oil in small nonstick skillet over medium heat. Add onion and cook, stirring occasionally, until softened, 2–3 minutes. Add garlic, cumin, and oregano; cook, stirring constantly, until fragrant, 30 seconds.

2 Stir in tomatillos, broth, and hominy; bring to boil. Reduce heat and simmer about 1 minute. Add shrimp and corn. Cover and cook, stirring occasionally, until shrimp are just opaque in center, 3–4 minutes. Stir in cilantro, salt, and pepper.

PER SERVING (generous 1 cup): 326 Cal, 9 g Total Fat, 1 g Sat Fat, 0 g Trans Fat, 210 mg Chol, 684 mg Sod, 34 g Carb, 9 g Sugar, 6 g Fib, 28 g Prot, 83 mg Calc.

8 PointsPlus® value

FOR YOUR° INFO

If you prefer this dish on the spicy side, add ½ teaspoon minced jalapeño or serrano pepper along with the garlic in step 1.

SCALLOPS WITH CAULIFLOWER, RAISINS, AND CAPERS

SERVES 1 UNDER 20 MINUTES

▲ **4 sea scallops (about 4 ounces)**

⅛ **teaspoon ground cumin**

⅛ **teaspoon salt**

⅛ **teaspoon black pepper**

2 **teaspoons olive oil**

▲ ½ **cup small (1-inch) cauliflower florets**

1 **tablespoon minced shallots**

2 **teaspoons golden raisins**

1 **teaspoon capers, minced**

▲ 3 **tablespoons reduced-sodium chicken broth**

1 Sprinkle scallops with cumin, salt, and pepper. Heat 1 teaspoon oil in small skillet over medium-high heat. Add scallops; cook, turning once, until just opaque in center, about 2 minutes. Transfer scallops to plate.

2 Add remaining 1 teaspoon oil to skillet. Add cauliflower, shallots, raisins, and capers. Cook, stirring constantly, until shallots are softened, about 2 minutes. Add broth; bring to boil. Cook, stirring often, until cauliflower is crisp-tender and most of liquid has evaporated, about 3 minutes. Serve cauliflower mixture with scallops.

PER SERVING (4 scallops and ⅓ cup cauliflower mixture): 231 Cal, 11 g Total Fat, 2 g Sat Fat, 0 g Trans Fat, 37 mg Chol, 590 mg Sod, 13 g Carb, 6 g Sugar, 2 g Fib, 21 g Prot, 52 mg Calc.

FOR YOUR INFO Smaller cauliflower florets cook quickly and evenly in this fast recipe. If you have a cauliflower with large florets, simply chop them into a smaller size.

FIVE-SPICE TOFU WITH EGGPLANT

SERVES 1   UNDER 20 MINUTES

1½ teaspoons canola oil

▲ 1 (6-ounce) Japanese eggplant, quartered lengthwise and cut into 1½-inch chunks

1 garlic clove, minced

⅛ teaspoon grated peeled fresh ginger

1 tablespoon water

2 teaspoons mirin

1 teaspoon reduced-sodium soy sauce

▲ 1 (¾-inch-thick) slice extra-firm tofu (¼-pound)

⅛ teaspoon five-spice powder

Pinch salt

Pinch black pepper

1 tablespoon chopped fresh cilantro

1 Heat 1 teaspoon oil in medium nonstick skillet over medium heat. Add eggplant and cook, stirring occasionally, until lightly browned, about 5 minutes. Add garlic and ginger; reduce heat and cook, stirring constantly, until fragrant, 30 seconds. Stir in water, mirin, and soy sauce. Cover and cook until eggplant is tender, about 1 minute. Transfer eggplant to plate and keep warm.

2 Meanwhile, sprinkle tofu with five-spice powder, salt, and pepper. Heat remaining ½ teaspoon oil in small nonstick skillet over medium heat. Add tofu and cook, turning once, until browned and heated through, 4–5 minutes. Transfer tofu to plate. Top with eggplant and sprinkle with cilantro.

PER SERVING (1 slice tofu and ¾ cup eggplant): 235 Cal, 13 g Total Fat, 1 g Sat Fat, 0 g Trans Fat, 0 mg Chol, 328 mg Sod, 18 g Carb, 7 g Sugar, 7 g Fib, 12 g Prot, 242 mg Calc.

STAY ON TRACK

Serve this speedy Asian dish with quick-cooking soba noodles (½ cup cooked 100% buckwheat soba noodles will increase the *PointsPlus* value by *2*).

You can double this recipe for an easy lunch later in the week.
EDAMAME–BLACK BEAN CHILI

EDAMAME–BLACK BEAN CHILI

SERVES 1

- 1 **teaspoon canola oil**
- ▲ 1 **small onion, diced**
- ▲ ½ **red bell pepper, diced**
- 1 **garlic clove, minced**
- ½ **teaspoon chili powder**
- ¼ **teaspoon cumin**
- ▲ 1 **cup canned diced fire-roasted tomatoes with green chiles**
- ▲ ½ **cup canned black beans, rinsed and drained**
- ▲ ⅓ **cup frozen shelled edamame**
- ▲ ⅓ **cup reduced-sodium vegetable or chicken broth**
- ▲ 2 **tablespoons plain fat-free Greek yogurt**
- ▲ 1 **tablespoon sliced scallion**

1 Heat oil in skillet over medium-high heat. Add onion and bell pepper. Cook, stirring occasionally, until vegetables are softened, 4–5 minutes. Add garlic, chili powder, and cumin; cook, stirring constantly, until fragrant, 30 seconds.

2 Add tomatoes, black beans, edamame, and broth; bring to boil. Reduce heat, cover, and simmer, stirring occasionally, until chili is slightly thickened, about 10 minutes. Serve chili topped with yogurt and scallion.

PER SERVING (generous 2 cups chili, 2 tablespoons yogurt, and 1 tablespoon scallion): 314 Cal, 8 g Total Fat, 0 g Sat Fat, 0 g Trans Fat, 0 mg Chol, 590 mg Sod, 45 g Carb, 14 g Sugar, 12 g Fib, 16 g Prot, 167 mg Calc.

7
PointsPlus®
value

CHAPTER 4

PETITE SWEETS

Treats to make and enjoy—plus
extras to share with friends.

ZUCCHINI-BUTTERSCOTCH MINI–BUNDT CAKES

MAKES 12

1¼ cups white whole wheat flour

1¼ teaspoons baking powder

¼ teaspoon salt

½ cup low-fat buttermilk

½ cup granulated sugar

¼ cup canola oil

¼ cup apple butter

▲ 1 large egg

1 teaspoon vanilla extract

▲ 1 cup shredded zucchini or carrots

3 tablespoons butterscotch morsels

Confectioners' sugar

1 Preheat oven to 400°F. Spray 12-cavity mini–Bundt pan with nonstick spray.

2 Stir together flour, baking powder, and salt in large bowl. Whisk together buttermilk, granulated sugar, oil, apple butter, egg, and vanilla in medium bowl. Add buttermilk mixture to flour mixture and stir just until blended. Stir in zucchini and butterscotch morsels. Fill prepared cavities evenly with batter.

3 Bake until tops of cakes spring back when lightly pressed, 12–15 minutes. Cool in pan on wire rack 10 minutes. Remove cakes from pan and let cool completely on rack. Dust with confectioners' sugar before serving.

PER SERVING (1 cake): 152 Cal, 6 g Total Fat, 1 g Sat Fat, 0 g Trans Fat, 18 mg Chol, 128 mg Sod, 22 g Carb, 11 g Sugar, 2 g Fib, 3 g Prot, 26 mg Calc.

STAY ON TRACK

Place remaining cakes in zip-close plastic bags. Store at room temperature up to 3 days or freeze up to 3 months. To serve, if frozen, thaw at room temperature. Dust with confectioners' sugar.

Butterscotch morsels are a welcome surprise in these tiny cakes.
ZUCCHINI-BUTTERSCOTCH MINI-BUNDT CAKES

CANDIED GINGER–CARDAMOM ANGEL FOOD CAKES

MAKES 2

⅓ **cup cake flour**

¼ **teaspoon ground cardamom**

▲ 2 **large egg whites**

¼ **teaspoon cream of tartar**

¼ **cup granulated sugar**

1 **teaspoon finely chopped candied ginger**

1 **teaspoon grated orange zest**

¼ **teaspoon vanilla extract**

Confectioners' sugar

1 Preheat oven to 375°F. Sift together flour and cardamom in small bowl.

2 With electric mixer on medium speed, beat egg whites and cream of tartar in large bowl until soft peaks form. Add granulated sugar, one tablespoon at a time, beating until egg whites form stiff, glossy peaks. Beat in ginger, orange zest, and vanilla.

3 Sift flour mixture, one third at a time, over egg whites, gently folding with rubber spatula just until well combined (do not overmix). Divide batter between 2 ungreased 4-inch mini–tube pans.

4 Bake until tops of cakes spring back when lightly pressed, 15–20 minutes. Invert pans on rack to cool 10 minutes. Run thin knife around edge of cakes to loosen from sides and center tubes of pans. Remove cakes from pans. Let cool completely on rack. Dust with confectioners' sugar before serving.

PER SERVING (1 cake): 171 Cal, 0 g Total Fat, 0 g Sat Fat, 0 g Trans Fat, 0 mg Chol, 56 mg Sod, 39 g Carb, 19 g Sugar, 1 g Fib, 6 g Prot, 12 mg Calc.

5
PointsPlus
value

STAY ON TRACK

Place remaining cake in zip-close plastic bag. Store at room temperature up to 3 days or freeze up to 3 months. To serve, if frozen, thaw at room temperature. Dust with confectioners' sugar.

BLOOD ORANGE SOUFFLÉS

MAKES 2

2 **teaspoons plus 2 tablespoons granulated sugar**

1 **teaspoon butter**

2 **teaspoons white whole wheat flour**

Zest and juice of 1 blood orange

▲ 2 **tablespoons fat-free milk**

1 **large egg yolk**

2 **teaspoons orange-flavored liqueur (optional)**

▲ 2 **egg whites**

¼ **teaspoon cream of tartar**

Confectioners' sugar

1 Preheat oven to 375°F. Spray 2 (6-ounce) ramekins or soufflé dishes with nonstick spray. Sprinkle 2 teaspoons granulated sugar into 1 ramekin, turning to coat bottom and side. Transfer excess sugar to second dish and turn to coat bottom and side. Refrigerate dishes until ready to use.

2 Melt butter in small saucepan over medium heat. Add flour and cook, stirring constantly, 1 minute. Whisk in orange juice and milk; bring to boil. Cook, whisking constantly, until orange juice mixture thickens, about 1 minute. Transfer juice mixture to large bowl. Let cool slightly. Stir in egg yolk, liqueur (if using), and orange zest.

3 Meanwhile, with electric mixer at medium speed, beat egg whites and cream of tartar in medium bowl until soft peaks form. Gradually beat in remaining 2 tablespoons granulated sugar until stiff peaks form. Stir one-fourth of beaten egg whites into orange juice mixture. With rubber spatula, gently fold in remaining egg whites just until no streaks of white remain.

4 Spoon batter into prepared ramekins. Place ramekins in small baking dish. Pour enough hot water in baking dish to come halfway up sides of ramekins. Bake until soufflés are golden brown and puffed, about 20 minutes. Carefully remove soufflés from water bath. Dust with confectioners' sugar and serve at once.

PER SERVING (1 soufflé): 176 Cal, 4 g Total Fat, 2 g Sat Fat, 0 g Trans Fat, 110 mg Chol, 80 mg Sod, 25 g Carb, 20 g Sugar, 1 g Fib, 6 g Prot, 47 mg Calc.

FOR YOUR INFO If blood oranges aren't available, use a Cara Cara orange or navel orange instead.

BROWNIE SWIRL CHEESECAKES

MAKES 12

CHEESECAKE LAYER

- **1** **(8-ounce) package fat-free cream cheese, softened**
- **¼** **cup sugar**
- ▲ **1** **large egg**
- **½** **teaspoon vanilla extract**
- **1** **ounce semisweet chocolate, chopped**
- ▲ **1** **tablespoon fat-free milk**

BROWNIE LAYER

- **¾** **cup white whole wheat flour**
- **⅓** **cup unsweetened cocoa**
- **1** **ounce semisweet chocolate, finely chopped**
- **¾** **teaspoon baking powder**
- **¼** **teaspoon salt**
- ▲ **1** **large egg**
- ▲ **1** **egg white**
- **¾** **cup sugar**
- **¼** **cup canola oil**
- **¼** **cup low-fat buttermilk**
- **1** **teaspoon vanilla extract**

1 Preheat oven to 350°F. Line 12 muffin cups with paper liners; spray liners with nonstick spray.

2 To make cheesecake layer, with electric mixer on medium speed, beat cream cheese in medium bowl until smooth, about 1 minute. Gradually add sugar, beating until fluffy, about 1 minute. Beat in egg and vanilla until blended. Transfer 3 tablespoons cheesecake batter to small bowl. Set aside remaining cheesecake batter.

3 Place chocolate and milk in small microwavable bowl; cover with wax paper. Microwave on High until chocolate melts, about 45 seconds. Stir until smooth. Stir chocolate mixture into reserved 3 tablespoons cheesecake batter until blended. Set aside chocolate batter.

4 To make brownie layer, stir together flour, cocoa, chocolate, baking powder, and salt in small bowl. Whisk together egg and egg white in medium bowl. Whisk in sugar, oil, buttermilk, and vanilla. Add flour mixture to egg mixture and stir until blended. Divide batter evenly among prepared muffin cups.

5 Top brownie layer evenly with reserved cheesecake batter. Drop reserved chocolate batter in small dollops over cheesecake batter. Swirl batter with wooden pick to create marbled effect.

6 Bake until tops are just set, 20–25 minutes. Let cool completely in pan on rack. Cover and refrigerate until chilled, at least 4 hours. Serve chilled.

PER SERVING (1 cheesecake): 178 Cal, 7 g Total Fat, 2 g Sat Fat, 0 g Trans Fat, 38 mg Chol, 237 mg Sod, 25 g Carb, 16 g Sugar, 2 g Fib, 6 g Prot, 87 mg Calc.

STAY ON TRACK

Wrap each remaining cheesecake in plastic wrap then in foil. Refrigerate up to 3 days or freeze up to 3 months. If frozen, thaw in the refrigerator. Serve at room temperature.

Top the cheesecakes with fresh raspberries for a special treat.
BROWNIE SWIRL CHEESECAKES

WHITE CHOCOLATE SOUFFLÉ WITH BRANDY SAUCE

MAKES 1

3 **teaspoons sugar**

½ **ounce white chocolate, chopped**

▲ 1 **teaspoon fat-free milk**

▲ 1 **large egg white**

¼ **teaspoon cream of tartar**

¼ **teaspoon vanilla extract**

1 **tablespoon vanilla frozen yogurt, softened**

½ **teaspoon brandy**

1 Preheat oven to 375°F. Spray (4-ounce) ramekin or soufflé dish with nonstick spray. Sprinkle 1 teaspoon sugar into ramekin, turning to coat bottom and side. Refrigerate dish until ready to use.

2 Place white chocolate and milk in small microwavable dish; cover with wax paper. Microwave on High until chocolate is melted, 10–15 seconds. Stir until smooth, then let cool slightly.

3 With electric mixer on medium speed, beat egg white and cream of tartar in medium bowl until soft peaks form, 1–2 minutes. Add remaining 2 teaspoons sugar and vanilla and beat until stiff peaks form. Fold chocolate mixture into beaten egg white just until combined. Spoon into prepared ramekin.

4 Place ramekin in small baking dish. Pour enough hot water in baking dish to come halfway up sides of ramekin. Bake until soufflé is golden brown and puffed, 12–15 minutes.

5 Meanwhile, to make sauce, stir together frozen yogurt and brandy in small bowl until melted and smooth. Carefully remove soufflé from water bath. Serve at once with sauce.

PER SERVING (1 soufflé and about 1 tablespoon sauce):
160 Cal, 5 g Total Fat, 3 g Sat Fat, 0 g Trans Fat, 11 mg Chol, 77 mg Sod, 22 g Carb, 21 g Sugar, 0 g Fib, 6 g Prot, 68 mg Calc.

4
PointsPlus®
value

STAY ON TRACK   Make this an even more indulgent dessert by serving it with fresh orange segments.

BANANAS FOSTER CUPCAKES

MAKES 4

CUPCAKES

- ⅔ **cup white whole wheat flour**
- ½ **teaspoon baking powder**
- ¼ **teaspoon salt**
- ¼ **teaspoon ground nutmeg**
- ⅛ **teaspoon baking soda**
- ▲ ½ **small ripe banana, mashed (about ¼ cup)**
- ⅓ **cup granulated sugar**
- ▲ ¼ **cup plain fat-free Greek yogurt**
- 1 **tablespoon canola oil**
- ▲ 1 **large egg**
- ½ **teaspoon vanilla extract**

FROSTING

- ½ **cup confectioners' sugar**
- 1 **teaspoon unsalted butter, melted**
- ½ **teaspoon dark rum or rum extract**
- ½ **teaspoon vanilla extract**
- ½ **teaspoon water**

1 Preheat oven to 375°F.

2 To make cupcakes, stir together flour, baking powder, salt, nutmeg, and baking soda in medium bowl. Whisk together mashed banana, granulated sugar, yogurt, oil, egg, and vanilla in small bowl. Add banana mixture to flour mixture and stir just until blended.

3 Place 4 (2 ½-inch) round ovenproof paper–baking cups on small baking sheet. (Note: Look for paper baking cups in the baking section of crafts stores and larger supermarkets.) Spoon batter into baking cups. Bake until toothpick inserted into centers comes out clean, 20–25 minutes. Transfer cupcakes to rack to cool completely.

4 Meanwhile, to make frosting, stir together confectioners' sugar, butter, rum, vanilla, and water in small bowl until combined. Spread frosting evenly over tops of cooled cupcakes.

PER SERVING (1 cupcake): 284 Cal, 6 g Total Fat, 1 g Sat Fat, 0 g Trans Fat, 56 mg Chol, 275 mg Sod, 52 g Carb, 34 g Sugar, 3 g Fib, 6 g Prot, 28 mg Calc.

7 PointsPlus® value

STAY ON TRACK Place the remaining cupcakes in an airtight container and cover. Refrigerate up to 4 days or freeze up to 3 months. To serve, if frozen, thaw at room temperature overnight.

ALMOND-BLUEBERRY CORNMEAL MUFFINS

MAKES 2

¼ **cup white whole wheat flour**

2 **tablespoons cornmeal**

¼ **teaspoon baking powder**

⅛ **teaspoon salt**

2 **tablespoons low-fat buttermilk**

2 **tablespoons granulated sugar**

▲ 1 **large egg**

½ **tablespoon canola oil**

1 **teaspoon grated orange zest**

▲ 2 **tablespoons fresh or frozen unsweetened blueberries**

1 **teaspoon turbinado (raw) sugar**

1 **teaspoon sliced almonds**

1 Preheat oven to 375°F.

2 Stir together flour, cornmeal, baking powder, and salt in medium bowl. Whisk together buttermilk, granulated sugar, egg, oil, and orange zest in small bowl. Add buttermilk mixture to flour mixture and stir just until blended. Stir in blueberries.

3 Place 2 (2½-inch) round ovenproof paper–baking cups on small baking sheet. (Note: Look for paper baking cups in the baking section of crafts stores and larger supermarkets.) Spoon batter into baking cups. Sprinkle tops with turbinado sugar and almonds. Bake until muffins are golden and toothpick inserted into centers comes out with a few moist crumbs attached, about 20 minutes. Transfer to rack to cool completely.

PER SERVING (1 muffin): 238 Cal, 7 g Total Fat, 1 g Sat Fat, 0 g Trans Fat, 108 mg Chol, 263 mg Sod, 38 g Carb, 16 g Sugar, 3 g Fib, 6 g Prot, 45 mg Calc.

6 PointsPlus® value

STAY ON TRACK

Place the remaining muffin in a heavy zip-close plastic bag. Store at room temperature up to 3 days or freeze up to 3 months. To serve, if frozen, thaw at room temperature overnight.

CHOCOLATE-CHERRY MINI-STRUDELS

MAKES 4

- **4 teaspoons finely chopped almonds**
- **1 teaspoon plus 1 tablespoon sugar**
- ▲ **1 cup fresh cherries, pitted or frozen unsweetened pitted cherries**
- **2 teaspoons water**
- **1 teaspoon cornstarch**
- **½ teaspoon cinnamon**
- **1 tablespoon chopped dark chocolate**
- **½ teaspoon almond extract**
- **2 (9 x 14-inch) sheets frozen phyllo dough, thawed**

1 Stir together almonds and 1 teaspoon sugar in small bowl.

2 Combine cherries, remaining 1 tablespoon sugar, water, cornstarch, and cinnamon in small nonstick skillet; set over medium-low heat. Cook, stirring frequently, until thick and syrupy, about 4 minutes. Remove from heat; stir in chocolate and almond extract. Transfer to small bowl and let cool slightly.

3 Preheat oven to 375°F. Spray small baking sheet with nonstick spray.

4 Place 1 phyllo sheet on work surface with short side facing you. (Keep remaining phyllo covered with damp paper towels and plastic wrap to keep it from drying out.) Lightly spray phyllo with nonstick spray. Cut phyllo sheet lengthwise in half. Sprinkle each phyllo half with ¾ teaspoon almond mixture; then spoon one-fourth of cherry filling over bottom half of each piece, leaving 1-inch border. Roll up, jelly-roll fashion. Repeat with remaining phyllo, 1½ teaspoons of remaining almond mixture, and remaining filling, making a total of 4 strudels.

5 Place strudels, seam side down, on prepared baking sheet. Lightly spray strudels with nonstick spray. Cut 3 (½-inch) slits in top of each strudel to allow steam to escape. Sprinkle tops of strudels with remaining almond mixture. Bake until phyllo is golden, about 12 minutes. Let cool completely on baking sheet on rack.

PER SERVING (2 strudels): 106 Cal, 3 g Total Fat, 2 g Sat Fat, 0 g Trans Fat, 0 mg Chol, 47 mg Sod, 20 g Carb,10 g Sugar, 2 g Fib, 1 g Prot, 14 mg Calc.

STAY ON TRACK Place the remaining strudels in a heavy zip-close plastic bag. Store at room temperature up to 2 days.

PEACH-RASPBERRY HAND PIES

MAKES 6

1 cup plus 1 teaspoon white whole wheat flour

4 tablespoons sugar

¼ teaspoon salt

2 tablespoons canola oil

1 tablespoon cold butter, cut into small pieces

3 tablespoons ice water

1 teaspoon apple cider vinegar

▲ 1 large peach, peeled, pitted, and diced

▲ ½ cup fresh raspberries

½ teaspoon cinnamon

▲ 1 tablespoon fat-free milk

1 To make crust, combine 1 cup flour, 1 tablespoon sugar, and salt in food processor; pulse until blended. Add oil and butter; pulse until mixture resembles fine crumbs. Combine water and vinegar in small bowl. Pour through feed tube, pulsing just until dough forms. Divide dough into 6 equal pieces. Shape each piece into disk. Wrap each disk in plastic wrap; refrigerate until chilled, about 20 minutes.

2 Preheat oven to 375°F. Line large baking sheet with parchment paper.

3 To make filling, toss together peach, raspberries, 2 tablespoons of remaining sugar, remaining 1 teaspoon flour, and cinnamon in medium bowl.

4 On lightly floured surface, roll out each disk of dough into 5-inch round. Spoon about 2 tablespoons filling on half of each round, leaving ½-inch border. Fold dough over filling to make half-moon shape. Crimp edges of dough with tines of fork to seal. Repeat with remaining dough and filling. Brush tops of pies with milk and sprinkle with remaining 1 tablespoon sugar. Place pies on prepared baking sheet.

5 Bake until pies are golden, about 25 minutes. Let cool on baking sheet 10 minutes. Transfer pies to wire rack to cool completely. Serve warm or at room temperature.

PER SERVING (1 hand pie): 178 Cal, 7 g Total Fat, 2 g Sat Fat, 0 g Trans Fat, 5 mg Chol, 112 mg Sod, 27 g Carb, 9 g Sugar, 4 g Fib, 3 g Prot, 10 mg Calc.

STAY ON TRACK Place the remaining pies in a heavy zip-close plastic bag. Freeze up to 3 months. To serve, thaw at room temperature overnight.

Make these in summer so you can use juicy local peaches.
PEACH-RASPBERRY HAND PIES

NECTARINE-RASPBERRY COBBLERS WITH LAVENDER

MAKES 4

▲ 1 **nectarine, pitted and chopped**

▲ ½ **cup fresh raspberries**

2 **tablespoons sugar**

1 **teaspoon dried lavender**

1 **teaspoon grated lemon zest**

1 **teaspoon lemon juice**

¼ **teaspoon cinnamon**

½ **cup reduced-fat baking mix**

▲ 3 **tablespoons fat-free milk**

1 Preheat oven to 400°F. Spray 4 (6-ounce) ovenproof ramekins or custard cups with nonstick spray.

2 Toss together nectarine, raspberries, sugar, lavender, lemon zest and juice, and cinnamon in medium bowl. Spoon into prepared ramekins.

3 To make topping, stir together baking mix and milk in small bowl until combined. Spoon evenly over fruit mixture. Place ramekins on small baking sheet. Bake until topping is golden and filling is bubbling, 15–18 minutes. Let cool 10 minutes to serve warm, or serve at room temperature.

PER SERVING (1 cobbler): 150 Cal, 2 g Total Fat, 1 g Sat Fat, 0 g Trans Fat, 0 mg Chol, 360 mg Sod, 30 g Carb, 11 g Sugar, 3 g Fib, 3 g Prot, 65 mg Calc.

STAY ON TRACK

Cover cobblers and refrigerate up to 2 days. To reheat, place cobbler on small baking sheet and cover loosely with foil. Bake at 400°F until filling is heated through, 15 minutes.

BERRY AND YOGURT–TOPPED BISCUITS

MAKES 4

- ¼ **cup plus 2 teaspoons white whole wheat flour**
- ¼ **cup cornmeal**
- 1 **tablespoon sugar**
- ¼ **teaspoon baking powder**
- ⅛ **teaspoon baking soda**
- **Pinch salt**
- 2 **tablespoons low-fat buttermilk**
- 1½ **tablespoons olive oil**
- 1 **teaspoon grated orange zest**
- ▲ 2 **cups mixed fresh berries, such as blueberries, raspberries, and blackberries**
- 4 **tablespoons lemon fat-free yogurt**

1 Preheat oven to 425°F.

2 Stir together flour, cornmeal, sugar, baking powder, baking soda, and salt in small bowl. Add buttermilk, oil, and orange zest; stir until soft dough forms.

3 Transfer dough to lightly floured surface; knead two or three times. Shape dough into 5-inch square; cut into 4 (2½-inch) squares. Place biscuits about 1 inch apart on small ungreased baking sheet.

4 Bake biscuits until tops are golden brown, 10–12 minutes. Transfer to rack to cool completely.

5 Place 1 biscuit on plate; top with ½ cup berries and 1 tablespoon yogurt.

PER SERVING (1 topped biscuit): 163 Cal, 6 g Total Fat, 1 g Sat Fat, 0 g Trans Fat, 0 mg Chol, 108 mg Sod, 27 g Carb, 10 g Sugar, 4 g Fib, 3 g Prot, 41 mg Calc.

STAY ON TRACK Place biscuits in zip-close plastic bag. Store at room temperature 3 days or freeze 3 months. To serve, if frozen, thaw at room temperature. Top each with ½ cup berries and 1 tablespoon yogurt.

*A sprinkle of pistachios
adds flavor and crunch.*
**STRAWBERRIES AND
CREAM TARTLETS**

STRAWBERRIES AND CREAM TARTLETS

MAKES 2

▲ ¼ cup fat-free milk

▲ 1 large egg

2 teaspoons sugar

1 teaspoon white whole wheat flour

Pinch salt

¼ teaspoon vanilla extract

2 (9 x 14-inch) sheets frozen phyllo dough, thawed

1 tablespoon vanilla fat-free yogurt

2 teaspoons apple jelly

▲ 6 medium strawberries, hulled and sliced

2 teaspoons finely chopped pistachios

1 To make filling, whisk together milk, egg, sugar, flour, and salt in small saucepan; set over medium-low heat. Cook, stirring constantly, until mixture thickens and coats back of spoon, about 4 minutes (do not boil). Remove saucepan from heat; stir in vanilla. Transfer filling to small bowl. Cover and refrigerate until chilled, about 20 minutes.

2 Meanwhile, preheat oven to 350°F. Spray 2 (4-inch) tart pans with removable bottoms with nonstick spray.

3 Place 1 phyllo sheet on clean, dry work surface. (Keep remaining phyllo covered with damp paper towels and plastic wrap to keep it from drying out.) Lightly spray phyllo with nonstick spray; cut into 8 (3½ x 4½-inch) rectangles. Gently place 1 rectangle into 1 prepared pan, pressing phyllo against sides and bottom of pan to form 1-inch-high rim. Repeat with remaining rectangles, placing corners at different angles to form 1-inch-high rim. Lightly spray with nonstick spray. Repeat with remaining phyllo sheet and remaining pan. Place pans on small baking sheet and bake until browned, about 10 minutes. Cool completely in pans on rack, gently pressing phyllo down in center if puffed.

4 Stir yogurt into chilled filling. Place jelly in small microwavable bowl; cover with wax paper and microwave on High until warm, about 20 seconds.

5 Remove phyllo crusts from pans and place on plates. Spoon filling into crusts, spreading evenly. Top with strawberries. Brush melted jelly over strawberries. Sprinkle with pistachios and serve at once.

PER SERVING (1 tartlet): 174 Cal, 5 g Total Fat, 1 g Sat Fat, 0 g Trans Fat, 112 mg Chol, 214 mg Sod, 26 g Carb, 12 g Sugar, 2 g Fib, 7 g Prot, 75 mg Calc.

CRANBERRY-ORANGE RICE PUDDING

MAKES 1 CUP

- ▲ 1 **cup fat-free milk**
- 1 **cup cooked long-grain white rice**
- ¼ **cup dried cranberries**
- 1 **tablespoon honey**
- 1 **teaspoon grated orange zest**
- ¼ **teaspoon vanilla extract**

1 Bring milk, rice, cranberries, and honey to boil in medium saucepan. Reduce heat and simmer, uncovered, stirring often, until pudding is thick and creamy, about 15 minutes.

2 Remove pudding from heat and stir in orange zest and vanilla. Let cool 10 minutes to serve warm, or cover and refrigerate until chilled.

PER SERVING (generous ½ cup): 213 Cal, 0 g Total Fat, 0 g Sat Fat, 0 g Trans Fat, 2 mg Chol, 53 mg Sod, 48 g Carb, 26 g Sugar, 2 g Fib, 6 g Prot, 158 mg Calc.

STAY ON TRACK The rice pudding may be kept refrigerated, covered, up to 3 days.

GREEN APPLE–DRIED CHERRY BREAD PUDDING

MAKES 2

- ▲ ⅓ cup fat-free milk
- ▲ 1 large egg
- 1 tablespoon sugar
- ¼ teaspoon vanilla extract
- ¼ teaspoon cinnamon
- 2 thin slices whole wheat bread, trimmed and cut into 1-inch cubes (about ¾ cup)
- ▲ 1 small Granny Smith apple, peeled and shredded
- 1 tablespoon dried cherries, coarsely chopped

1 Preheat oven to 375°F. Spray 2 (6-ounce) ramekins or custard cups with nonstick spray.

2 Whisk together milk, egg, sugar, vanilla, and cinnamon in large bowl. Stir in bread cubes, apple, and cherries. Let stand 15 minutes, stirring occasionally. Spoon mixture evenly into prepared ramekins. Place ramekins on small baking sheet.

3 Bake until lightly puffed and knife inserted in centers comes out clean, 25–30 minutes. Let cool 10 minutes to serve warm, or serve at room temperature.

PER SERVING (1 dish): 189 Cal, 3 g Total Fat, 1 g Sat Fat, 0 g Trans Fat, 108 mg Chol, 183 mg Sod, 32 g Carb, 18 g Sugar, 4 g Fib, 8 g Prot, 101 mg Calc.

STAY ON TRACK

Cover the remaining bread pudding with plastic wrap. Refrigerate up to 2 days. To serve, cover with wax paper and microwave on High until heated through, 1–2 minutes.

ALMOND CRÈME CARAMEL

MAKES 2

3	**tablespoons sugar**
2	**tablespoons water**
½	**cup vanilla-flavored almond milk**
¼	**cup low-fat half-and-half**
▲ **1**	**large egg**
½	**teaspoon vanilla extract**
	Pinch salt

1 Preheat oven to 350°F.

2 Combine 2 tablespoons sugar and water in small heavy-bottomed saucepan; set over medium heat. Cook, shaking pan occasionally, until mixture turns to amber color, 5–7 minutes. Immediately pour caramel into 2 (6-ounce) ovenproof ramekins or custard cups. Carefully tilt ramekins to coat bottoms and about halfway up sides (sugar mixture is very hot). Let stand until caramel is cool, about 10 minutes.

3 Meanwhile, bring almond milk and half-and-half just to simmer in small saucepan over medium heat. Whisk together egg, remaining 1 tablespoon sugar, vanilla, and salt in medium bowl. Gradually whisk hot almond-milk mixture into egg mixture. Pour mixture into prepared ramekins and place in small baking pan. Pour enough hot water in pan to come halfway up sides of ramekins. Bake until custards are just set around edges and still jiggle in center, 35–40 minutes.

4 Transfer ramekins to rack and let cool. Cover and refrigerate until custard is well chilled and set, at least 4 hours. Run thin knife around edge of ramekin to loosen custard. Unmold custard onto rimmed plate.

PER SERVING (1 custard): 118 Cal, 3 g Total Fat, 1 g Sat Fat, 0 g Trans Fat, 109 mg Chol, 182 mg Sod, 19 g Carb, 17 g Sugar, 0 g Fib, 4 g Prot, 40 mg Calc.

STAY ON TRACK — Cover the remaining custard in the ramekin with plastic wrap, and refrigerate up to 1 day.

VANILLA BEAN CRÈME BRÛLÉE

MAKES 2

¼ **vanilla bean, split lengthwise**

▲ ⅔ **cup fat-free milk**

▲ 1 **large egg**

2 **tablespoons plus 2 teaspoons sugar**

1 Preheat oven to 325°F.

2 With small, sharp knife, split vanilla bean lengthwise in half and scrape out seeds. Discard vanilla bean. Combine vanilla bean seeds and milk in small saucepan; set over medium heat. Bring to boil. Remove from heat.

3 Meanwhile, whisk together egg and 2 tablespoons sugar in medium bowl until pale yellow, about 30 seconds. Slowly whisk hot milk mixture into egg mixture until blended. Divide mixture evenly between 2 (4-ounce) ovenproof ramekins or custard cups. Place ramekins in small baking pan. Add enough hot water to pan to come halfway up sides of ramekins. Bake until custards are just set around edges and centers still jiggle slightly, about 25 minutes.

4 Transfer ramekins to rack and let cool. Cover and refrigerate until the custard is thoroughly chilled and set, at least 4 hours.

5 To serve, preheat broiler. Sprinkle 1 custard with 1 teaspoon of remaining sugar. Place ramekin on baking sheet and broil, 4 inches from heat, until sugar is melted and bubbling, 3–4 minutes. Let stand until topping is crisp, 2–3 minutes.

PER SERVING (1 crème brûlée): 103 Cal, 2 g Total Fat, 1 g Sat Fat, 0 g Trans Fat, 109 mg Chol, 67 mg Sod, 17 g Carb, 16 g Sugar, 0 g Fib, 6 g Prot, 112 mg Calc.

STAY ON TRACK The baked crème brûlée may be kept refrigerated in the ramekin, covered, up to 1 day. When ready to serve, continue with step 5.

PEAR CLAFOUTI

MAKES 2

▲ **1** **large ripe Bartlett pear, cored and thinly sliced**

▲ **⅓** **cup fat-free milk**

Grated zest of 1 lemon

1 **tablespoon white whole wheat flour**

1 **tablespoon granulated sugar**

▲ **1** **large egg**

1 **teaspoon unsalted butter, melted**

¼ **teaspoon cinnamon**

Confectioners' sugar for dusting

1 Preheat oven to 375°F. Spray 2 (6-ounce) baking dishes with nonstick spray.

2 Arrange half of pear slices in concentric circles, overlapping slightly, into each prepared baking dish.

3 Whisk together milk, lemon zest, flour, granulated sugar, egg, butter, and cinnamon in medium bowl. Pour mixture evenly over pear slices. Place baking dishes on small baking sheet.

4 Bake until puffed and golden, about 30 minutes. Let cool 10 minutes to serve warm, or serve at room temperature. Dust with confectioners' sugar just before serving.

PER SERVING (1 dish): 166 Cal, 4 g Total Fat, 2 g Sat Fat, 0 g Trans Fat, 113 mg Chol, 51 mg Sod, 29 g Carb, 18 g Sugar, 5 g Fib, 5 g Prot, 83 mg Calc.

STAY ON TRACK Cover the remaining clafouti in the baking dish with plastic wrap. Refrigerate up to 1 day. Serve chilled or at room temperature. Dust with confectioners' sugar just before serving.

You can make this simple, satisfying dessert with apples, too.
PEAR CLAFOUTI

STRAWBERRY SWIRL SEMIFREDDO

MAKES 1½ CUPS

▲ 1 **cup strawberries, coarsely chopped**

2 **teaspoons strawberry fruit spread**

▲ 1 **cup fat-free ricotta cheese**

1 **tablespoon plus 1 teaspoon confectioners' sugar**

Grated zest of 1 orange

¼ **cup thawed frozen fat-free whipped topping**

1 Stir together strawberries and fruit spread in medium bowl. Let stand 5 minutes.

2 Meanwhile, combine ricotta, confectioners' sugar, and orange zest in food processor; puree. Transfer to medium bowl. Stir in strawberry mixture. Gently fold in whipped topping just until blended. Cover and refrigerate until well chilled, at least 2 hours.

PER SERVING (generous ¾ cup): 170 Cal, 0 g Total Fat, 0 g Sat Fat, 0 g Trans Fat, 10 mg Chol, 166 mg Sod, 25 g Carb, 16 g Sugar, 2 g Fib, 17 g Prot, 426 mg Calc.

STAY ON TRACK — The semifreddo may be kept refrigerated, covered, up to 2 days.

RASPBERRY-LEMON MOUSSE PARFAIT

MAKES 2

- ▲ 1 **cup fresh raspberries**
- 2 **teaspoons granulated sugar**
- ▲ ¾ **cup fat-free ricotta cheese**
- 3 **tablespoons confectioners' sugar**
- **Grated zest of 2 lemons**
- 3 **tablespoons warm water**
- 2 **teaspoons powdered egg whites or meringue powder**
- ¼ **cup thawed frozen fat-free whipped topping**

1 Stir together raspberries and granulated sugar in small bowl. Let stand, stirring once or twice, until sugar has completely dissolved and juices are syrupy, about 15 minutes.

2 Meanwhile, combine ricotta, 2 tablespoons confectioners' sugar, and lemon zest in food processor; puree. Transfer to medium bowl.

3 Stir together water, powdered egg whites, and remaining 1 tablespoon confectioners' sugar in medium bowl until powdered egg whites are completely dissolved. With electric mixer on medium speed, beat egg white mixture until stiff peaks form.

4 With rubber spatula, gently fold beaten egg whites into ricotta mixture just until blended. Gently fold in whipped topping. Alternately layer ricotta mixture and raspberry mixture into 2 parfait glasses.

PER SERVING (1 parfait): 193 Cal, 0 g Total Fat, 0 g Sat Fat, 0 g Trans Fat, 8 mg Chol, 128 mg Sod, 31 g Carb, 21 g Sugar, 5 g Fib, 17 g Prot, 337 mg Calc.

STAY ON TRACK

Cover the remaining parfait with plastic wrap. Refrigerate up to 2 days.

CHOCOLATE-ESPRESSO SORBET

MAKES 4 CUPS

- ▲ **4 cups fat-free half-and-half**
- **⅔ cup sugar**
- **¼ cup dark chocolate chips**
- **3 tablespoons unsweetened cocoa**
- **1 tablespoon instant espresso powder**
- **1 teaspoon vanilla extract**
- **2 tablespoons chocolate-covered espresso beans, coarsely chopped**

1 Combine half-and-half, sugar, chocolate chips, cocoa, and espresso powder in large saucepan; set over medium heat. Cook, stirring constantly, until sugar has dissolved and chocolate is melted, about 5 minutes. Remove saucepan from heat; stir in vanilla. Transfer to large bowl to cool to room temperature, about 45 minutes.

2 Pour mixture into ice-cream maker and freeze according to manufacturer's instructions, adding chopped espresso beans about 10 minutes before sorbet is done. Transfer sorbet to freezer container and freeze until firm, at least 4 hours.

PER SERVING (½ cup): 178 Cal, 3 g Total Fat, 2 g Sat Fat, 0 g Trans Fat, 0 mg Chol, 101 mg Sod, 32 g Carb, 25 g Sugar, 1 g Fib, 5 g Prot, 164 mg Calc.

STAY ON TRACK The sorbet may be frozen up to 2 months.

BANANA–WHITE CHOCOLATE PUDDING POPS

MAKES 8

▲ 2½ cups fat-free milk

¼ cup sugar

3 tablespoons white whole wheat flour

2 teaspoons grated peeled fresh ginger

Pinch salt

¼ cup white chocolate chips

1 teaspoon vanilla extract

Pinch ground nutmeg

▲ 2 medium bananas, mashed

1 Whisk together milk, sugar, flour, ginger, and salt in medium saucepan until smooth; set over medium-low heat. Cook, whisking constantly, until mixture comes to boil and thickens, about 5 minutes. Remove from heat. Add white chocolate chips, vanilla, and nutmeg and stir until smooth.

2 Combine bananas and half of milk mixture in food processor; puree. Add banana mixture to saucepan and stir to combine.

3 Divide mixture among 8 (3-ounce) ice pop molds. Freeze until completely frozen, at least 6 hours.

PER SERVING (1 ice pop): 109 Cal, 2 g Total Fat, 1 g Sat Fat, 0 g Trans Fat, 3 mg Chol, 56 mg Sod, 21 g Carb, 15 g Sugar, 1 g Fib, 4 g Prot, 108 mg Calc.

STAY ON TRACK The ice pops may be frozen up to 2 months.

WHITE CHOCOLATE–IRISH CREAM FONDUE WITH STRAWBERRIES

MAKES 8 TABLESPOONS FONDUE   UNDER 20 MINUTES

¼ cup low-fat half-and-half

¼ cup chopped white chocolate

1 tablespoon Irish cream liqueur

▲ ¾ cup strawberries, per serving, hulled

1 Bring half-and-half to boil in small saucepan over medium-high heat. Remove from heat. Add white chocolate and liqueur and stir until mixture is smooth.

2 Spoon 2 tablespoons fondue into small bowl; serve with ¾ cup strawberries.

PER SERVING (2 tablespoons fondue with ¾ cup strawberries): 111 Cal, 4 g Total Fat, 2 g Sat Fat, 0 g Trans Fat, 15 mg Chol, 26 mg Sod, 17 g Carb, 13 g Sugar, 2 g Fib, 2 g Prot, 58 mg Calc.

STAY ON TRACK

Transfer fondue to a container and cover. Refrigerate up to 1 week. To reheat, place 2 tablespoons fondue in a bowl; cover and microwave until warm. Serve with ¾ cup strawberries.

MIXED BERRY GRATIN

MAKES 1   UNDER 20 MINUTES

▲ ½   **cup plain fat-free Greek yogurt**

3   **teaspoons packed brown sugar**

1   **teaspoon grated lime zest**

▲ 1   **cup fresh or thawed frozen unsweetened mixed berries**

1 Preheat broiler.

2 Combine yogurt, 2 teaspoons brown sugar, and lime zest in small bowl. Place berries in shallow flameproof 12- or 16-ounce baking dish. Spoon yogurt mixture over berries. Sprinkle with remaining 1 teaspoon brown sugar.

3 Broil 4 inches from heat until berries are warm and topping is browned and bubbling, 6–8 minutes. Serve warm or at room temperature.

PER SERVING (1 gratin): 173 Cal, 1 g Total Fat, 0 g Sat Fat, 0 g Trans Fat, 0 mg Chol, 46 mg Sod, 35 g Carb, 29 g Sugar, 4 g Fib, 11 g Prot, 109 mg Calc.

FOR YOUR INFO Instead of the berries, you can use almost any fresh seasonal fruit for this recipe: Sliced plums, pears, peaches, and apricots all work well.

MACADAMIA NUT MACAROONS

MAKES 20

▲ 2 **large egg whites, at room temperature**

¼ **cup sugar**

3 **tablespoons almond paste**

Grated zest of 1 lemon

1 **(7-ounce) package shredded sweetened coconut**

1 **tablespoon finely chopped macadamia nuts**

1 Preheat oven to 325°F. Line large rimmed baking sheet with parchment paper.

2 Combine egg whites, sugar, almond paste, and lemon zest in food processor; puree. Add coconut and pulse until combined.

3 Drop dough, by tablespoonfuls, onto prepared baking sheet 1-inch apart, making total of 20 cookies. Sprinkle tops of cookies with nuts. Bake until macaroons are lightly golden around edges, 25 minutes. Cool on baking sheet 15 minutes. With spatula, transfer macaroons to rack and cool completely.

PER SERVING (1 cookie): 72 Cal, 5 g Total Fat, 3 g Sat Fat, 0 g Trans Fat, 0 mg Chol, 37 mg Sod, 8 g Carb, 7 g Sugar, 0 g Fib, 1 g Prot, 7 mg Calc.

STAY ON TRACK

Place the macaroons in an airtight container with sheets of wax paper between layers and cover. Store at room temperature up to 1 week.

Treat yourself to a sweet with one of these tiny indulgences.

MACADAMIA NUT MACAROONS

PINEAPPLE-CARROT STREUSEL BARS, PAGE 158

MAPLE-WALNUT PRALINES, PAGE 159

PINEAPPLE-CARROT STREUSEL BARS

MAKES 20

2	cups white whole wheat flour
½	cup packed light brown sugar
½	teaspoon cinnamon
½	teaspoon baking soda
¼	teaspoon salt
⅓	cup canola oil
▲ 1	large egg
▲ 1	(8-ounce) can unsweetened crushed pineapple, drained
▲ 1	medium carrot, shredded
¼	cup apricot fruit spread
¼	cup old-fashioned oats
1	tablespoon coarsely chopped walnuts

1 Preheat oven to 350°F. Spray 9-inch square baking pan with nonstick spray.

2 Place flour, brown sugar, cinnamon, baking soda, and salt in food processor; pulse until combined. Add oil and egg; pulse until mixture is crumbly.

3 Reserve ½ cup dough. Transfer remaining dough to prepared baking pan and press to form an even layer. Bake until lightly browned at edges, about 15 minutes.

4 Meanwhile, stir together pineapple, carrot, and fruit spread in medium bowl. Spread evenly over warm crust. Add oats and nuts to reserved dough; stir to combine. Crumble over top of pineapple mixture. Bake until topping is lightly browned, about 15 minutes. Let cool completely in pan on wire rack. Cut into 20 bars.

PER SERVING (1 bar): 135 Cal, 5 g Total Fat, 0 g Sat Fat, 0 g Trans Fat, 11 mg Chol, 68 mg Sod, 20 g Carb, 9 g Sugar, 2 g Fib, 2 g Prot, 11 mg Calc.

STAY ON TRACK

Place the bars in a single layer in an airtight container and cover. Refrigerate up to 3 days or freeze up to 1 month. To serve, if frozen, thaw at room temperature overnight.

MAPLE-WALNUT PRALINES

MAKES 16

¾ **cup light brown sugar**

▲ ½ **cup fat-free milk**

1 **tablespoon dark corn syrup**

1 **tablespoon maple syrup**

¼ **teaspoon baking soda**

¾ **cup toasted walnuts, coarsely chopped**

2 **teaspoons unsalted butter**

2 **teaspoons vanilla extract**

1 Stir together sugar, milk, corn syrup, maple syrup, and baking soda in medium heavy-bottomed saucepan. Bring to boil over medium-high heat. Reduce heat and simmer, stirring occasionally, until candy thermometer reads 234°F, 12–15 minutes. Remove from heat.

2 Stir in walnuts, butter, and vanilla. Drop mixture, by tablespoonfuls, onto wax paper, making 16 pralines. Let stand until set, about 20 minutes.

PER SERVING (1 praline): 90 Cal, 4 g Total Fat, 1 g Sat Fat, 0 g Trans Fat, 1 mg Chol, 28 mg Sod, 13 g Carb, 12 g Sugar, 0 g Fib, 1 g Prot, 25 mg Calc.

3 PointsPlus® value

STAY ON TRACK

Place the pralines in an airtight container with sheets of wax paper between layers and cover. Store at room temperature up to 1 week.

DOUBLE ORANGE–DARK CHOCOLATE TRUFFLES

MAKES 30

---

8 ounces dark chocolate chips

⅓ cup low-fat half-and-half

2 tablespoons butter

Grated zest of 1 orange

1 tablespoon orange-flavored liqueur

⅓ cup unsweetened cocoa

1 Combine chocolate chips, half-and-half, and butter in medium microwavable bowl. Cover with wax paper and microwave on High, stirring halfway through cooking time, until chocolate is melted and smooth, about 1 minute. Stir in orange zest and liqueur. Let cool to room temperature. Cover with plastic wrap. Refrigerate until chocolate mixture is firm, at least 3 hours or up to 2 days.

2 Put cocoa in small bowl. Dust hands with cocoa. Divide truffle mixture into 30 portions. Quickly roll each portion into 1-inch ball, then roll in cocoa to coat evenly.

PER SERVING (1 truffle): 49 Cal, 3 g Total Fat, 2 g Sat Fat, 0 g Trans Fat, 2 mg Chol, 9 mg Sod, 6 g Carb, 3 g Sugar, 1 g Fib, 0 g Prot, 8 mg Calc.

STAY ON TRACK Place the truffles in an airtight container with sheets of wax paper between layers and cover. Refrigerate up to 1 week. Bring to room temperature before serving.

CHOCOLATE-PECAN MINI MERINGUES

MAKES 72

½ cup toasted pecans

▲ 4 large egg whites, at room temperature

¼ teaspoon cream of tartar

1 cup sugar

1 tablespoon unsweetened cocoa powder

1 teaspoon vanilla extract

1 Preheat oven to 400°F. Spray 2 baking sheets lightly with nonstick spray.

2 Place pecans in food processor and process until finely ground. Set aside.

3 With electric mixer on medium speed, beat egg whites and cream of tartar in large bowl until soft peaks form. Add granulated sugar, one tablespoon at a time, beating until egg whites form stiff, glossy peaks. Beat in cocoa powder and vanilla. With rubber spatula, gently fold in pecans.

4 Transfer egg white mixture to large zip-close plastic bag with one corner snipped off. Pipe 72 mounds (each about 1 rounded tablespoon) onto baking sheets. Place in oven and reduce heat to 250°F. Bake until meringues are dried and crisped, about 1 hour. Remove from oven and cool completely on baking sheets.

PER SERVING (3 meringues): 51 Cal, 2 g Total Fat, 0 g Sat Fat, 0 g Trans Fat, 0 mg Chol, 9 mg Sod, 9 g Carb, 9 g Sugar, 0 g Fib, 1 g Prot, 2 mg Calc.

Place the meringues in an airtight container and store at room temperature up to 3 weeks.

CHAPTER 5

MEALS WITH LEFTOVERS

These hearty dishes make enough for a meal now plus three to store and savor later.

HOISIN BEEF AND VEGETABLE STEW

SERVES 1 PLUS LEFTOVERS

▲ 1 **pound lean boneless sirloin steak, trimmed and cut into ½-inch cubes**

½ **cup dry white wine**

▲ 1 **cup reduced-sodium beef broth**

¼ **cup hoisin sauce**

▲ 6 **carrots, cut diagonally into 1½-inch chunks**

▲ 1 **(10-ounce) package cremini mushrooms, halved**

▲ 1½ **cups thawed frozen pearl onions**

▲ 1 **red bell pepper, cut into 1-inch pieces**

¼ **teaspoon salt**

1 **tablespoon cornstarch**

Chopped fresh cilantro

▲ **Thinly sliced scallion**

1 Spray large saucepan with nonstick spray and set over medium-high heat. Add half of beef; cook, stirring often, until browned, about 4 minutes. Transfer beef to plate. Repeat with remaining beef.

2 Add wine to saucepan and stir to scrape up browned bits from bottom of pan. Return beef and any accumulated juices to pan. Stir in ¾ cup broth and hoisin sauce; bring to boil. Cover, reduce heat, and simmer 20 minutes. Add carrots, mushrooms, onions, bell pepper, and salt. Cover, return to simmer, and cook until beef and vegetables are tender, about 20 minutes.

3 Stir together remaining ¼ cup broth and cornstarch in small bowl until smooth. Add to saucepan and cook, stirring constantly, until stew thickens, about 3 minutes.

4 To serve, ladle 1½ cups stew into bowl; sprinkle with cilantro and scallion.

PER SERVING (1 ½ cups): 315 Cal, 6 g Total Fat, 2 g Sat Fat, 0 g Trans Fat, 50 mg Chol, 551 mg Sod, 27 g Carb, 11 g Sugar, 5 g Fib, 31 g Prot, 70 mg Calc.

STORE AND SERVE LATER

Let the remaining stew cool completely. Divide the stew among three airtight containers and cover. Refrigerate up to 4 days or freeze up to 3 months. To reheat one serving, if frozen, thaw stew in the refrigerator overnight. Transfer to a small saucepan. Cover and cook over medium heat, stirring occasionally, until heated through, about 5 minutes.

If you like a spicy stew, add a pinch of crushed red pepper.
HOISIN BEEF AND VEGETABLE STEW

CHILE-BRAISED BEEF AND BLACK BEAN STEW

SERVES 1 PLUS LEFTOVERS

5	**whole dried guajillo chiles, seeded and torn into large pieces**
▲ 1	**cup reduced-sodium chicken broth**
3	**garlic cloves, peeled**
2	**tablespoons apple cider vinegar**
1½	**teaspoons dried oregano**
1½	**teaspoons ground cumin**
½	**teaspoon salt**
2	**teaspoons olive oil**
▲ ¾	**pound lean boneless sirloin steak, trimmed and cut into ½-inch cubes**
▲ 1	**large onion, chopped**
▲ 1	**cup canned black beans, rinsed and drained**
▲ 2	**zucchini (12 ounces), cut into ¾-inch chunks**

1 Place chiles in medium skillet. Set over medium-low heat and toast, turning often, until fragrant, about 3 minutes. Place in medium bowl. Cover with boiling water and let stand 10 minutes.

2 Drain chilies and place in blender. Add ½ cup broth, garlic, vinegar, oregano, cumin, and salt; puree.

3 Heat oil in large saucepan over medium-high heat. Add half of beef and cook, stirring occasionally, until browned, about 4 minutes. Transfer beef to plate. Repeat with remaining beef. Add onion to saucepan and cook, stirring often, until softened, 5 minutes.

4 Stir in chile mixture, beef and any accumulated juices, and remaining ½ cup broth. Bring to boil. Cover, reduce heat, and simmer 35 minutes. Stir in beans and zucchini; cook, uncovered, until zucchini is tender, 5 minutes.

5 To serve, ladle 1½ cups stew into bowl.

PER SERVING (1½ cups): 363 Cal, 7 g Total Fat, 2 g Sat Fat, 0 g Trans Fat, 37 mg Chol, 575 mg Sod, 38 g Carb, 3 g Sugar, 5 g Fib, 31 g Prot, 125 mg Calc.

8 PointsPlus® value

STORE AND SERVE LATER

Let the remaining stew cool completely. Divide the stew among three airtight containers and cover. Refrigerate up to 4 days or freeze up to 3 months. To reheat one serving, if frozen, thaw stew in the refrigerator overnight. Transfer to a small saucepan. Cover and cook over medium heat, stirring occasionally, until heated through, about 5 minutes.

BEEF AND WINTER SQUASH TAGINE

SERVES 1 PLUS LEFTOVERS

2 teaspoons olive oil

▲ ¾ pound lean boneless sirloin steak, trimmed and cut into ½-inch cubes

▲ 1 large onion, coarsely chopped

▲ 1 cup reduced-sodium beef broth

3 garlic cloves, chopped

2 teaspoons smoked paprika

2 teaspoons ground cumin

¼ teaspoon pumpkin pie spice

▲ 1 (14 ½-ounce) can diced tomatoes with basil and oregano

1 (1-inch) piece fresh ginger, peeled and cut into matchstick strips

▲ 3 cups cubed (¾-inch) peeled calabaza or butternut squash (about 1 pound)

2 teaspoons honey

¼ teaspoon salt

Chopped fresh mint

1 Heat oil in large saucepan over medium-high heat. Add half of beef and cook, stirring occasionally, until browned, about 4 minutes. Transfer beef to plate. Repeat with remaining beef. Add onion and ¼ cup broth. Cook, stirring to scrape up browned bits from bottom of pan, until onion is softened, 5 minutes.

2 Add garlic, paprika, cumin, and pumpkin pie spice. Cook, stirring constantly, until fragrant, 30 seconds. Stir in tomatoes, ginger, and remaining ¾ cup broth; bring to boil. Cover, reduce heat, and simmer 25 minutes. Add squash, honey, and salt. Cover, return to simmer, and cook until squash is tender, about 12 minutes.

3 To serve, ladle 1½ cups tagine into bowl; sprinkle with mint.

PER SERVING (1½ cups): 255 Cal, 7 g Total Fat, 2 g Sat Fat, 0 g Trans Fat, 37 mg Chol, 411 mg Sod, 26 g Carb, 9 g Sugar, 4 g Fib, 23 g Prot, 106 mg Calc.

STORE AND SERVE LATER

Let the remaining tagine cool completely. Divide the tagine among three airtight containers and cover. Refrigerate up to 4 days or freeze up to 3 months. To reheat one serving, if frozen, thaw tagine in the refrigerator overnight. Transfer to a small saucepan. Cover and cook over medium heat, stirring occasionally, until heated through, about 5 minutes. Sprinkle with chopped fresh mint.

BEEF, BARLEY, AND SHIITAKE MUSHROOM CASSEROLE

SERVES 1   PLUS LEFTOVERS

- ▲ ¾ **pound ground lean beef (7% fat or less)**
- ▲ 2 **carrots, sliced**
- ▲ 1 **medium onion, chopped**
- ▲ 1 **red bell pepper, chopped**
- ▲ 4 **ounces shiitake mushrooms, stems removed and caps sliced**
- ▲ 1 **(10-ounce) package frozen chopped kale, thawed and drained**
- ▲ ½ **cup quick-cooking barley**
- ▲ 1 **(14 ½-ounce) can reduced-sodium beef broth**
-   2 **tablespoons minced fresh thyme**
-   ½ **teaspoon salt**
-   ¾ **cup shredded fontina cheese**
-   2 **tablespoons grated Parmesan cheese**

1 Preheat oven to 350°F.

2 Spray large ovenproof skillet with nonstick spray and set over medium-high heat. Add beef, carrots, onion, bell pepper, and mushrooms. Cook, breaking apart beef with wooden spoon, until beef is browned, about 5 minutes. Stir in kale, barley, broth, thyme, and salt; bring to boil. Cover and place in oven. Bake until barley is tender, 25–30 minutes.

3 Uncover and sprinkle with fontina and Parmesan. Bake, uncovered, until cheese is melted, about 5 minutes.

4 To serve, spoon 2 cups casserole onto plate.

PER SERVING (2 cups): 367 Cal, 13 g Total Fat, 7 g Sat Fat, 0 g Trans Fat, 77 mg Chol, 609 mg Sod, 33 g Carb, 6 g Sugar, 8 g Fib, 31 g Prot, 284 mg Calc.

STORE AND SERVE LATER

Let the remaining casserole cool completely. Spoon into an airtight container and cover. Refrigerate up to 4 days. To reheat one serving, transfer 2 cups of casserole to medium microwavable dish. Cover with wax paper and microwave on High until heated through, about 2 minutes.

SHORTCUT BEEF AND SPINACH CANNELLONI

SERVES 1 PLUS LEFTOVERS

- 8 (6 x 3-inch) no-boil lasagna noodles
- 1 teaspoon olive oil
- ▲ ¾ pound ground lean beef (7% fat or less)
- ▲ 1 onion, finely chopped
- 1 teaspoon dried basil
- ½ teaspoon salt
- ¼ teaspoon ground nutmeg
- ▲ 1 (10-ounce) package frozen leaf spinach, thawed and squeezed dry
- 1 cup shredded reduced-fat Italian cheese blend
- 2 teaspoons red-wine vinegar
- 1½ cups fat-free marinara sauce
- ¼ cup water

1 Preheat oven to 425°F. Spray 9 x 13-inch baking dish with nonstick spray.

2 Fill large bowl with hot water. Add noodles and let stand 10 minutes. Drain.

3 Meanwhile, heat oil in large nonstick skillet over medium heat. Add beef, onion, basil, salt, and nutmeg. Cook, breaking apart beef with wooden spoon, until beef is browned, about 6 minutes. Add spinach and cook, stirring often, until liquid has evaporated, about 3 minutes. Transfer to medium bowl and let cool slightly. Stir in ½ cup Italian cheese blend and vinegar.

4 Stir together ½ cup marinara sauce and ¼ cup water in prepared baking dish; spread evenly in dish. Working with one noodle at time, cut noodle in half crosswise. Spoon 1½ tablespoons beef mixture down center of noodle. Roll up lengthwise and place, seam side down, in prepared baking dish. Repeat with remaining noodles and beef mixture. Spoon remaining sauce over noodles; sprinkle with remaining ½ cup cheese.

5 Cover and bake until noodles are tender, about 25 minutes. Let stand 10 minutes before serving.

6 To serve, transfer 4 cannelloni to plate.

PER SERVING (4 cannelloni): 424 Cal, 12 g Total Fat, 6 g Sat Fat, 0 g Trans Fat, 66 mg Chol, 994 mg Sod, 44 g Carb, 4 g Sugar, 7 g Fib, 35 g Prot, 345 mg Calc.

11 PointsPlus® value

STORE AND SERVE LATER

Let the remaining cannelloni cool completely. Transfer cannelloni to an airtight container and cover. Refrigerate up to 4 days. To reheat one serving, transfer 4 cannelloni to microwavable dish. Cover with wax paper and microwave on High until heated through, about 2 minutes.

SAGE-ROASTED PORK WITH SQUASH, APPLES, AND FIGS

SERVES 1 PLUS LEFTOVERS

▲ 1   **(1-pound) piece lean boneless pork loin, trimmed**

¾   **teaspoon ground coriander**

¾   **teaspoon dried sage**

½   **teaspoon salt**

1   **teaspoon olive oil**

▲ 1   **small (1-pound) butternut squash, peeled, seeded, and cut in 1-inch chunks (3 cups)**

▲ 2   **Golden Delicious apples, cored and cut into ¾-inch chunks**

6   **dried figs, quartered**

1   **cup apple cider**

2   **tablespoons brandy**

1   **(1-inch) strip orange zest, cut into thin strips**

1   **teaspoon red-wine vinegar**

1 Preheat oven to 375°F. Spray large roasting pan with nonstick spray.

2 Sprinkle pork with coriander, sage, and ¼ teaspoon salt. Heat oil in large skillet over medium-high heat. Add pork and cook, turning occasionally, until browned on all sides, about 7 minutes. Transfer pork to center of prepared roasting pan. Arrange squash, apples, and figs around pork.

3 Combine cider, brandy, orange zest, and remaining ¼ teaspoon salt in small skillet. Bring to boil over medium-high heat. Cook, stirring often, until reduced to ½ cup, about 4 minutes. Pour cider mixture over squash mixture in roasting pan; stir to coat.

4 Roast, stirring squash mixture once, until instant-read thermometer inserted in center of pork registers 145°F and squash mixture is tender, 30–35 minutes. Let stand 10 minutes. Stir vinegar into squash mixture. Cut pork into 12 slices.

5 To serve, place 3 slices pork and 1 cup squash mixture on plate.

PER SERVING (3 slices pork and 1 cup squash mixture):
296 Cal, 3 g Total Fat, 1 g Sat Fat, 0 g Trans Fat, 74 mg Chol, 362 mg Sod, 40 g Carb, 27 g Sugar, 6 g Fib, 25 g Prot, 77 mg Calc.

STORE AND SERVE LATER

Let the remaining pork and squash mixture cool completely. Keeping pork and squash mixture separate, place each into three separate airtight containers and cover. Refrigerate up to 4 days or freeze up to 3 months. To reheat one serving, if frozen, thaw pork and squash in the refrigerator overnight. Transfer 3 slices pork and 1 cup squash mixture to microwavable dish. Cover with wax paper and microwave on High until heated through, about 2 minutes.

LEMON-MUSTARD ROASTED PORK WITH FENNEL AND ONIONS

SERVES 1 PLUS LEFTOVERS

2 tablespoons Dijon mustard

2 tablespoons honey

2 teaspoons grated lemon zest

▲ 2 large carrots, quartered lengthwise and cut into 2-inch sticks

▲ 1 large fennel bulb, thinly sliced

▲ 1 large sweet onion, thinly sliced

1¼ teaspoons fennel seeds, crushed

¼ teaspoon salt

1½ teaspoons olive oil

▲ 1 (1-pound) lean pork tenderloin, trimmed

3 tablespoons light sour cream

1 Preheat oven to 425°F.

2 Stir together mustard, honey, and lemon zest in medium bowl. Place carrots, fennel bulb, onion, 1 teaspoon fennel seeds, and salt in large roasting pan. Drizzle with oil; toss to coat. Arrange vegetables in single layer; cover and bake 10 minutes.

3 Uncover pan. Toss vegetables and move toward edges of pan. Place pork in center of pan. Brush with 1 tablespoon mustard mixture; sprinkle with remaining ¼ teaspoon fennel seeds. Roast, uncovered, until instant-read thermometer inserted into center of pork registers 145°F and vegetables are tender, about 20 minutes. Let stand 10 minutes.

4 To make sauce, stir sour cream into remaining mustard mixture. Cut pork into 12 slices.

5 To serve, place 3 slices pork and 1¼ cup vegetables on plate; drizzle with generous 1 tablespoon sauce.

PER SERVING (3 slices pork, 1¼ cups vegetables, and generous 1 tablespoon sauce): 250 Cal, 6 g Total Fat, 2 g Sat Fat, 0 g Trans Fat, 78 mg Chol, 451 mg Sod, 23 g Carb, 12 g Sugar, 4 g Fib, 26 g Prot, 81 mg Calc.

6 PointsPlus® value

STORE AND SERVE LATER

Let the remaining pork and vegetables cool completely. Place in an airtight container and cover. Cover sauce. Refrigerate up to 4 days. To reheat one serving, transfer 3 slices pork and 1¼ cup vegetables to microwavable dish. Cover with wax paper and microwave on High until heated through, about 2 minutes. Drizzle with generous 1 tablespoon of the sauce.

BAKED PORK CHOPS WITH MANGO CHUTNEY–YOGURT SAUCE

SERVES 1   PLUS LEFTOVERS

¼ **cup mango chutney**

▲ ¼ **cup plain fat-free Greek yogurt**

▲ 1 **scallion, chopped**

1 **teaspoon grated peeled fresh ginger**

2 **teaspoons all-purpose flour**

¼ **teaspoon salt**

▲ 4 **(5-ounce) lean boneless center-cut pork loin chops, trimmed**

▲ 1 **mango, peeled, pitted, and diced**

1 Preheat oven to 375°F. Spray 9 x 13-inch baking dish with nonstick spray.

2 Stir together chutney, yogurt, scallion, ginger, flour, and ⅛ teaspoon salt in small bowl. Sprinkle pork chops with remaining ⅛ teaspoon salt; place in prepared baking dish. Spoon chutney sauce over chops and spread to cover. Bake until instant-read thermometer inserted into side of each chop registers 145°F, about 20 minutes. Sprinkle mango over sauce; bake until mango is heated through, about 3 minutes.

3 To serve, place 1 pork chop and about ¼ cup sauce on plate.

PER SERVING (1 pork chop and about ¼ cup sauce):
250 Cal, 6 g Total Fat, 2 g Sat Fat, 0 g Trans Fat, 78 mg Chol, 451 mg Sod, 23 g Carb, 12 g Sugar, 4 g Fib, 26 g Prot, 81 mg Calc.

6 PointsPlus© value

STORE AND SERVE LATER

Let the remaining pork and sauce cool completely. Divide the pork and sauce among three airtight containers. Cover and refrigerate up to 4 days. To reheat one serving, transfer 1 pork chop and about ¼ cup sauce to microwavable dish. Cover with wax paper and microwave on High until heated through, about 2 minutes.

*Serve the pork with steamed
pea shoots or spinach.*
**SMOKY PORK TENDERLOIN
WITH CHERRY-CABERNET SAUCE**

SMOKY PORK TENDERLOIN WITH CHERRY-CABERNET SAUCE

SERVES 1 PLUS LEFTOVERS

- ▲ 1 **(1-pound) lean pork tenderloin, trimmed**
- 1 **teaspoon olive oil**
- 2 **teaspoons smoked paprika**
- ½ **teaspoon salt**
- ⅔ **cup Cabernet or other dry red wine**
- ▲ ½ **cup reduced-sodium chicken broth**
- ¼ **cup dried tart cherries, chopped**
- 3 **tablespoons dark brown sugar**
- ▲ 2 **scallions, finely chopped**
- ▲ 1 **cup thawed frozen unsweetened dark cherries, coarsely chopped**
- 1 **tablespoon balsamic vinegar**
- ⅛ **teaspoon ground allspice**
- 1 **tablespoon cold water**
- 1 **teaspoon cornstarch**

1 Preheat oven to 425°F.

2 Place pork in small roasting pan and brush with oil. Sprinkle with paprika and ¼ teaspoon salt. Roast until instant-read thermometer inserted in center of pork registers 145°F, about 20 minutes. Let stand 10 minutes. Cut pork into 12 slices.

3 Meanwhile, combine wine, broth, dried cherries, brown sugar, and scallions in small saucepan. Set over medium-high heat and bring to boil. Cook, stirring occasionally, until reduced by one third, about 5 minutes. Stir in dark cherries, vinegar, allspice, and remaining ¼ teaspoon salt. Return to boil and cook, stirring occasionally, 3 minutes. Stir together water and cornstarch in small bowl until smooth; add to saucepan. Cook, stirring constantly, until sauce thickens, about 2 minutes. Remove from heat.

4 To serve, place 3 slices pork on plate; top with ⅓ cup sauce.

PER SERVING (3 slices pork and ⅓ cup sauce): 261 Cal, 4 g Total Fat, 1 g Sat Fat, 0 g Trans Fat, 74 mg Chol, 364 mg Sod, 23 g Carb, 17 g Sugar, 3 g Fib, 25 g Prot, 25 mg Calc.

6 PointsPlus® value

STORE AND SERVE LATER

Let the remaining pork and sauce cool completely. Keeping pork and sauce separate, place each into three separate airtight containers and cover. Refrigerate up to 4 days or freeze up to 3 months. To reheat one serving, if frozen, thaw pork and sauce in the refrigerator overnight. Transfer 3 slices pork to microwavable dish; drizzle with ⅓ cup sauce. Cover with wax paper and microwave on High until heated through, about 2 minutes.

ORANGE-CHIPOTLE GLAZED RIBS

SERVES 1 PLUS LEFTOVERS

Grated zest and juice of 1 navel orange

¾ cup apricot jam

2 tablespoons white-wine vinegar

1 tablespoon ketchup

2 teaspoons minced chipotles en adobo

2 teaspoons chili powder

¼ teaspoon ground allspice

¼ teaspoon salt

1½ pounds pork spareribs, trimmed (about 8 ribs)

1 Preheat oven to 350°F. Line rimmed baking sheet with foil.

2 To make sauce, stir together orange zest and juice, jam, vinegar, ketchup, chipotles, ½ teaspoon chili powder, allspice, and salt in small saucepan. Bring to boil over medium heat. Reduce heat and simmer, stirring occasionally, until slightly thickened, about 3 minutes (makes 1¼ cups). Set aside ½ cup sauce for serving.

3 Place ribs on prepared baking sheet; sprinkle with remaining 1½ teaspoons chili powder. Brush ribs with half of remaining sauce in saucepan. Bake 1 hour. Brush ribs with remaining sauce in saucepan and bake until tender, 30 minutes longer.

4 To serve, place 2 ribs on plate; drizzle with 2 tablespoons reserved sauce.

PER SERVING (2 ribs and 2 tablespoons sauce): 483 Cal, 24 g Total Fat, 9 g Sat Fat, 0 g Trans Fat, 96 mg Chol, 310 mg Sod, 44 g Carb, 29 g Sugar, 1 g Fib, 24 g Prot, 64 mg Calc.

STORE AND SERVE LATER

Let the remaining ribs cool completely. Divide ribs and sauce among three airtight containers (2 ribs and about 2 tablespoons sauce in each container) and cover. Refrigerate up to 4 days or freeze up to 2 months. To reheat one serving, if frozen, thaw in the refrigerator overnight. Transfer to microwavable dish; cover with wax paper and microwave on High until heated through, about 2 minutes.

Sweet, spicy, and saucy, these ribs will have you licking your fingers. **ORANGE-CHIPOTLE GLAZED RIBS**

FETA, TOMATO, AND PINE NUT–STUFFED CHICKEN BREASTS

SERVES 1 PLUS LEFTOVERS

▲ ⅓ cup bulgur

1 cup boiling water

⅓ cup sun-dried tomatoes (not oil-packed), chopped

¼ cup crumbled feta cheese

2 tablespoons pine nuts, toasted

¾ teaspoon dried oregano

▲ 4 (5-ounce) skinless boneless chicken breasts

¼ teaspoon salt

¼ teaspoon black pepper

2 teaspoons olive oil

Lemon wedges

1 To make filling, place bulgur in medium bowl. Pour boiling water over bulgur; cover and let stand 25 minutes. Drain and return to bowl. Add tomatoes, feta, pine nuts, and ½ teaspoon oregano; stir to combine.

2 Preheat oven to 350°F.

3 Holding knife parallel to cutting board, against one long side of chicken breast, cut chicken almost in half, leaving ½-inch "hinge" (do not cut all the way through). Open breast and spread flat like a book. Repeat with remaining chicken. Cover with plastic wrap and pound to ¼-inch thickness.

4 Top each breast with one-fourth of filling. Roll up each breast from short side and secure with wooden toothpicks. Sprinkle with remaining ¼ teaspoon oregano, salt, and pepper.

5 Heat oil in large ovenproof skillet over medium-high heat. Add chicken and cook, turning occasionally, until browned, about 5 minutes. Transfer skillet to oven and bake until chicken is cooked through, about 12 minutes. Transfer chicken to cutting board and let stand 5 minutes.

6 Remove toothpicks from 1 chicken breast and cut into slices. Transfer to plate and serve with lemon wedges.

PER SERVING (1 stuffed chicken breast): 278 Cal, 11 g Total Fat, 3 g Sat Fat, 0 g Trans Fat, 87 mg Chol, 417 mg Sod, 13 g Carb, 2 g Sugar, 3 g Fib, 33 g Prot, 75 mg Calc.

7 PointsPlus® value

STORE AND SERVE LATER

Let the remaining chicken breasts cool completely. Divide the chicken among three airtight containers and cover. Refrigerate up to 4 days or freeze up to 4 months. To reheat one serving, if frozen, thaw in the refrigerator overnight. Transfer the chicken to a microwavable dish. Cover with wax paper and microwave on High until heated through, about 2 minutes. Remove toothpicks and cut the chicken into slices. Serve with lemon wedges.

ROSEMARY CHICKEN STEW WITH WHITE BEANS AND OLIVES

SERVES 1   PLUS LEFTOVERS

- **2** **teaspoons olive oil**
- **1** **pound boneless skinless chicken thighs, cut in 1-inch chunks**
- **1** **cup dry white wine**
- ▲ **2** **leeks, halved and chopped, white and light green parts only**
- **2** **garlic cloves, minced**
- ▲ **1** **(19-ounce) can cannellini (white kidney) beans, rinsed and drained**
- ▲ **1** **(14½-ounce) can diced tomatoes with basil and oregano**
- **1½** **teaspoons chopped fresh rosemary**
- **¼** **teaspoon salt**
- **¼** **teaspoon red pepper flakes**
- ▲ **1** **large zucchini, halved lengthwise and sliced**
- **¼** **cup kalamata olives, pitted and chopped**

1 Heat oil in large saucepan over medium-high heat. Add chicken and cook, stirring occasionally, until browned, about 6 minutes. Add wine, leeks, and garlic; bring to boil. Cook until leeks are softened, 5 minutes.

2 Add beans, tomatoes, rosemary, salt, and pepper flakes; return to boil. Cover, reduce heat, and simmer 10 minutes. Add zucchini and olives; cover and simmer until zucchini is tender, about 5 minutes.

3 To serve, ladle 1¾ cups stew into bowl.

PER SERVING (1¾ cups): 433 Cal, 13 g Total Fat, 3 g Sat Fat, 0 g Trans Fat, 74 mg Chol, 897 mg Sod, 37 g Carb, 8 g Sugar, 9 g Fib, 31 g Prot, 132 mg Calc.

10 PointsPlus® value

STORE AND SERVE LATER

Let the remaining stew cool completely. Divide the stew among three airtight containers and cover. Refrigerate up to 4 days or freeze up to 4 months. To reheat one serving, if frozen, thaw stew in the refrigerator overnight. Transfer to a small saucepan. Cover and cook over medium heat, stirring occasionally, until heated through, about 5 minutes.

ASIAN CHICKEN SUCCOTASH

SERVES 1 PLUS LEFTOVERS

2 teaspoons canola oil

▲ 1 pound boneless skinless chicken breasts, cut into ¾-inch chunks

2 garlic cloves, thinly sliced

1 tablespoon peeled chopped fresh ginger

▲ 1 cup reduced-sodium chicken broth

¾ cup water

▲ 1½ cups frozen corn kernels

▲ 1 large red bell pepper, chopped

▲ 2 jalapeño peppers, seeded and diced

▲ 3 small zucchini (about 1 pound), chopped

▲ 1 cup shelled edamame

1½ tablespoons reduced-sodium soy sauce

Chopped fresh cilantro

Lime wedges

1 Heat oil in large saucepan over medium heat. Add chicken, garlic, and ginger. Cook, stirring often, until chicken is lightly browned, about 6 minutes.

2 Add broth, water, corn, bell pepper, and jalapeños; bring to boil. Reduce heat and simmer 10 minutes. Add zucchini, edamame, and soy sauce. Cook, stirring occasionally, until zucchini is tender, 5 minutes.

3 To serve, spoon 1½ cups succotash into bowl. Sprinkle with cilantro and serve with lime wedges.

PER SERVING (1½ cups): 275 Cal, 8 g Total Fat, 1 g Sat Fat, 0 g Trans Fat, 63 mg Chol, 220 mg Sod, 22 g Carb, 4 g Sugar, 4 g Fib, 31 g Prot, 53 mg Calc.

STORE AND SERVE LATER

Let the remaining succotash cool completely. Divide the succotash among three airtight containers and cover. Refrigerate up to 4 days or freeze up to 4 months. To reheat one serving, if frozen, thaw succotash in the refrigerator overnight. Transfer to a small saucepan. Cover and cook over medium heat, stirring occasionally, until heated through, about 5 minutes. Sprinkle with cilantro and serve with lime wedges.

Ginger and soy sauce put an Asian spin on a Southern favorite. **ASIAN CHICKEN SUCCOTASH**

FIVE-SPICE BRAISED CHICKEN WITH PLUMS

SERVES 1 PLUS LEFTOVERS

▲ 4   purple plums

4   bone-in skinless chicken thighs (about 1½ pounds)

½   teaspoon salt

1   teaspoon olive oil

▲ 3   carrots, coarsely chopped

▲ 1   large red onion, chopped

¾   cup dry red wine

▲ ¾   cup reduced-sodium chicken broth

2   tablespoons honey

½   teaspoon dried thyme leaves

½   teaspoon five-spice powder

1 Cut 3 plums into wedges; chop remaining plum. Set aside.

2 Sprinkle chicken with ¼ teaspoon salt. Heat oil in large skillet over medium-high heat. Add chicken and cook, turning once, until browned, about 6 minutes. Transfer chicken to plate. Add carrots, onion, and remaining ¼ teaspoon salt to skillet; cook, stirring occasionally, until vegetables are softened, 5 minutes.

3 Add wine and chopped plum to skillet. Bring to boil and cook, stirring occasionally, 4 minutes. Stir in broth, honey, thyme, and five-spice powder; then add chicken and any accumulated juices. Return to boil. Cover, reduce heat, and simmer until chicken is tender, 15 minutes.

4 Add plum wedges to skillet. Cover and simmer until plums are softened, about 5 minutes.

5 To serve, transfer 1 chicken thigh to plate; top with about 1 cup plum sauce.

PER SERVING (1 chicken thigh and 1 cup plum sauce): 340 Cal, 12 g Total Fat, 3 g Sat Fat, 0 g Trans Fat, 86 mg Chol, 419 mg Sod, 26 g Carb, 19 g Sugar, 3 g Fib, 26 g Prot, 50 mg Calc.

STORE AND SERVE LATER

Let the remaining chicken and plum sauce cool completely. Divide the chicken and sauce among three airtight containers and cover. Refrigerate up to 4 days or freeze up to 4 months. To reheat one serving, if frozen, thaw in the refrigerator overnight. Transfer to a microwavable dish. Cover with wax paper and microwave on High until heated through, about 2 minutes.

TURKEY AND RED LENTIL MEAT LOAVES

SERVES 1   PLUS LEFTOVERS

2   **teaspoons canola oil**

▲ **1**   **onion, finely chopped**

▲ **1**   **large carrot, shredded**

1   **cup water**

▲ **¼**   **cup red lentils, picked over and rinsed**

1   **garlic clove, minced**

▲ **1**   **pound ground skinless turkey breast**

¼   **cup dried bread crumbs**

▲ **1**   **large egg**

1   **teaspoon Italian seasoning**

½   **teaspoon salt**

1 Preheat oven to 350°F. Line rimmed baking sheet with foil; spray foil with nonstick spray.

2 Heat oil in medium saucepan over medium heat. Add onion and carrot; cook, stirring often, until softened, 5 minutes. Add water, lentils, and garlic; bring to boil. Reduce heat and simmer until lentils are tender, but still hold their shape, about 12 minutes. Drain; transfer lentil mixture to bowl to cool slightly.

3 Add turkey, bread crumbs, egg, Italian seasoning, and salt to lentil mixture. Stir to combine. Shape into 4 (2 x 4-inch) oval loaves. Place on foil on prepared baking sheet.

4 Bake until instant-read thermometer inserted into side of each loaf registers 165°F, about 25 minutes.

5 To serve, place 1 meat loaf on plate.

PER SERVING (1 meat loaf): 248 Cal, 6 g Total Fat, 1 g Sat Fat, 0 g Trans Fat, 99 mg Chol, 444 mg Sod, 17 g Carb, 4 g Sugar, 3 g Fib, 34 g Prot, 39 mg Calc.

STORE AND SERVE LATER

Let the remaining meat loaves cool completely. Place the meat loaves in an airtight container and cover. Refrigerate up to 4 days or freeze up to 4 months. To reheat one serving, if frozen, thaw in the refrigerator overnight. Transfer one meat loaf to microwavable dish. Cover with wax paper and microwave on High until heated through, about 2 minutes.

SAUSAGE AND ARTICHOKE–STUFFED MUSHROOMS

SERVES 1 PLUS LEFTOVERS

▲ **4 large portobello mushrooms**

8 ounces Italian-style turkey sausage, casings removed

▲ **1½ cups thawed frozen artichokes, chopped**

▲ **1 small red onion, finely chopped**

▲ **½ large red bell pepper, chopped**

1 teaspoon dried basil

2 teaspoons red-wine vinegar

¼ teaspoon black pepper

3 tablespoons fresh whole wheat bread crumbs

¼ cup plus 2 tablespoons grated Romano cheese

1 Preheat oven to 425°F. Spray 9 x 13-inch baking dish with nonstick spray.

2 Remove stems from mushrooms. Using small spoon, scrape out and discard dark gills from underside of caps. Set mushrooms, stem side up, in prepared baking dish. Bake until mushrooms are softened, about 12 minutes.

3 Meanwhile, spray large skillet with nonstick spray; set over medium heat. Add sausage, artichokes, onion, bell pepper, and basil. Cook, breaking apart sausage with spoon, until vegetables are softened, about 8 minutes. Stir in vinegar and black pepper; remove from heat. Stir in bread crumbs and ¼ cup Romano.

4 Spoon sausage mixture onto mushroom caps, mounding in center. Bake until stuffing is hot and mushrooms are tender, about 12 minutes. Sprinkle with remaining 2 table-spoons Romano and bake until cheese is melted, about 2 minutes longer.

5 To serve, transfer 1 stuffed mushroom to plate.

PER SERVING (1 stuffed mushroom): 245 Cal, 11 g Total Fat, 2 g Sat Fat, 0 g Trans Fat, 45 mg Chol, 700 mg Sod, 19 g Carb, 6 g Sugar, 8 g Fib, 19 g Prot, 214 mg Calc.

6 PointsPlus value

STORE AND SERVE LATER

Let the remaining mushrooms cool completely. Place the mushrooms in an airtight container and cover. Refrigerate up to 4 days or freeze up to 4 months. To reheat one serving, if frozen, thaw in the refrigerator overnight. Transfer 1 mush-room to a microwavable plate. Cover with wax paper and microwave on High until heated through, about 2 minutes.

FISH STEW WITH CHORIZO AND GREENS

SERVES 1 PLUS LEFTOVERS

- 1 **teaspoon olive oil**
- ▲ 1 **red onion, chopped**
- 2 **ounces chorizo sausage, chopped**
- 2 **garlic cloves, minced**
- 1 **teaspoon Italian seasoning**
- ▲ 1 **green bell pepper, chopped**
- ▲ 1 **(10-ounce) package frozen chopped kale, thawed**
- ▲ 1 **(14½-ounce) can stewed tomatoes**
- ▲ 1 **(14½-ounce) can diced tomatoes**
- 1 **cup water**
- ▲ 1 **pound cod fillets, cut into 1-inch chunks**
- 2 **teaspoons smoked paprika**
- ¾ **teaspoon hot pepper sauce**
- ¼ **teaspoon salt**

1 Heat oil in large saucepan over medium heat. Add onion and cook, stirring often, until softened, 5 minutes. Add chorizo, garlic, and Italian seasoning; cook, stirring often, 2 minutes.

2 Add bell pepper, kale, stewed tomatoes, diced tomatoes, and water. Bring to boil, breaking apart stewed tomatoes with wooden spoon. Cover, reduce heat, and simmer until kale is tender, 15 minutes.

3 Add cod, paprika, pepper sauce, and salt. Cover, return to simmer, and cook until cod is just opaque in center, about 3 minutes.

4 To serve, ladle 2 cups stew into bowl.

PER SERVING (2 cups): 250 Cal, 8 g Total Fat, 2 g Sat Fat, 0 g Trans Fat, 56 mg Chol, 877 mg Sod, 20 g Carb, 9 g Sugar, 5 g Fib, 26 g Prot, 175 mg Calc.

STORE AND SERVE LATER

Let the remaining stew cool completely. Divide the stew among three airtight containers and cover. Refrigerate up to 4 days or freeze up to 3 months. To reheat one serving, if frozen, thaw stew in the refrigerator overnight. Transfer to a small saucepan. Cover and cook over medium heat, stirring occasionally, until heated through, about 5 minutes.

CAJUN SALMON–SWEET POTATO CHOWDER

SERVES 1   PLUS LEFTOVERS

1   teaspoon olive oil

▲ 2   carrots, chopped

▲ 1   onion, chopped

▲ 1   celery stalk, chopped

▲ 1   red bell pepper, chopped

1   teaspoon salt-free Cajun seasoning

▲ 2   sweet potatoes (¾ pound), peeled and cut into ¾-inch chunks

▲ 1   (14½-ounce) can reduced-sodium chicken broth

1   cup water

1   (1-pound) skinless salmon fillet, cut into 1-inch chunks

▲ 1   cup fresh or thawed frozen corn kernels

▲ ¾   cup fat-free half-and-half

⅓   cup chopped fresh basil or parsley

¼   teaspoon salt

1   Heat oil in large saucepan over medium heat. Add carrots, onion, and celery. Cook, stirring occasionally, until vegetables are softened, 5 minutes. Add bell pepper and Cajun seasoning; cook, stirring occasionally, 2 minutes.

2   Add sweet potatoes, broth, and water; bring to boil. Cover, reduce heat, and simmer until potatoes are tender, 10 minutes. Add salmon and corn; simmer until salmon is just opaque in center, about 3 minutes.

3   Reduce heat to low. Add half-and-half, basil, and salt. Cook, stirring often, just until heated through, about 1 minute longer.

4   To serve, ladle 1¾ cups chowder into bowl.

PER SERVING (1¾ cups): 366 Cal, 11 g Total Fat, 2 g Sat Fat, 0 g Trans Fat, 72 mg Chol, 490 mg Sod, 17 g Carb, 12 g Sugar, 6 g Fib, 32 g Prot, 136 mg Calc.

STORE AND SERVE LATER

Let the remaining chowder cool completely. Divide the chowder among three airtight containers and cover. Refrigerate up to 4 days. To reheat one serving, transfer to a small saucepan. Cover and cook over medium heat, stirring occasionally, until heated through, about 5 minutes.

Fat-free half-and-half stands in for cream in this satisfying soup.
CAJUN SALMON–SWEET POTATO CHOWDER

SHRIMP AND ROASTED RED PEPPER PAELLA

SERVES 1   PLUS LEFTOVERS

2	teaspoons olive oil
▲ 1	large onion, chopped
▲ 3	ounces lean reduced-sodium ham, diced
2	garlic cloves, chopped
▲ 2	cups reduced-sodium chicken broth
1	cup water
1⅓	cups arborio rice
▲ 1	cup chopped roasted red bell peppers (not oil-packed)
1	teaspoon smoked paprika
½	teaspoon saffron threads, crumbled
¼	teaspoon black pepper
▲ 1	pound large peeled and deveined shrimp
¼	cup green olives, pitted and chopped
¼	cup chopped fresh flat-leaf parsley
	Lemon wedges

1 Heat oil in large saucepan over medium heat. Add onion and cook, stirring often, until softened, 5 minutes. Add ham and garlic; cook, stirring constantly, 1 minute.

2 Add broth, water, rice, bell peppers, paprika, saffron, and black pepper; bring to simmer. Cover, reduce heat, and simmer until rice is almost tender, about 15 minutes.

3 Stir in shrimp and olives. Cover and simmer over low heat until rice is tender and shrimp are just opaque in center, about 5 minutes longer. Remove from heat; stir in parsley.

4 To serve, spoon 2 cups paella onto plate; serve with lemon wedges.

PER SERVING (2 cups): 428 Cal, 7 g Total Fat, 1 g Sat Fat, 0 g Trans Fat, 179 mg Chol, 659 mg Sod, 60 g Carb, 3 g Sugar, 5 g Fib, 31 g Prot, 77 mg Calc.

11
PointsPlus®
value

STORE AND SERVE LATER
Let the remaining paella cool completely. Spoon paella into an airtight container and cover. Refrigerate up to 4 days. To reheat one serving, transfer 2 cups paella to medium microwavable dish. Cover with wax paper and microwave on High until heated through, about 2 minutes.

GREEK SPINACH AND FETA STRATA

SERVES 1 PLUS LEFTOVERS

- **2** teaspoons olive oil
- ▲ **4** scallions, thinly sliced
- **2** garlic cloves, minced
- ▲ **2** (10-ounce) packages frozen chopped spinach, thawed and squeezed dry
- **6** oil-packed sun-dried tomatoes, drained, patted dry with paper towels, and chopped
- **⅛** teaspoon ground nutmeg
- ▲ **6** large egg whites
- **1** cup low-fat (1%) milk
- **½** cup reduced-fat (2%) cottage cheese
- **1** tablespoon spicy brown mustard
- **¼** teaspoon salt
- **4** slices whole wheat sandwich bread, cut into cubes
- **½** cup crumbled reduced-fat feta cheese
- **⅓** cup chopped fresh dill

1 Spray 9-inch square baking dish with nonstick spray.

2 Heat oil in large nonstick skillet over medium heat. Add scallions and garlic; cook, stirring often, until softened, 2 minutes. Add spinach, tomatoes, and nutmeg. Cook, stirring occasionally, until spinach is tender, about 4 minutes. Transfer to large bowl and let cool slightly.

3 Whisk together egg whites, milk, cottage cheese, mustard, and salt in large bowl.

4 Place half of bread cubes in prepared baking dish. Top with half of spinach mixture, half of feta, and half of dill. Ladle half of cottage cheese mixture into dish. Top with remaining bread cubes, spinach, feta, and dill. Add remaining cottage cheese mixture. Let stand 30 minutes.

5 Preheat oven to 375°F. Bake strata until top is lightly browned and knife inserted in center comes out clean, 45 minutes. Let stand 10 minutes. Cut into 4 squares.

6 To serve, transfer 1 square to plate.

PER SERVING (1 square): 260 Cal, 8 g Total Fat, 3 g Sat Fat, 0 g Trans Fat, 11 mg Chol, 868 mg Sod, 25 g Carb, 7 g Sugar, 7 g Fib, 24 g Prot, 382 mg Calc.

6 PointsPlus® value

STORE AND SERVE LATER

Let the remaining strata cool completely. Cover the strata in the baking dish and refrigerate up to 4 days. To reheat one serving, transfer 1 square to a microwavable plate. Cover with wax paper and microwave on High until heated through, about 2 minutes.

You can make this with small acorn squash instead of butternut squash.
PICADILLO-STUFFED BUTTERNUT SQUASH

PICADILLO-STUFFED BUTTERNUT SQUASH

SERVES 1 PLUS LEFTOVERS

▲ **2** **small butternut squash (2 pounds total), halved lengthwise and seeded**

2 **teaspoons canola oil**

▲ **1** **large onion, chopped**

▲ **1** **green bell pepper, chopped**

▲ **2** **cups frozen soy crumbles**

1 **tablespoon chili powder**

2 **teaspoons ground cumin**

1 **cup water**

▲ **1** **(8-ounce) can tomato sauce**

⅓ **cup raisins, minced**

¼ **cup pitted green olives, chopped**

2 **tablespoons red-wine vinegar**

2 **teaspoons Worcestershire sauce**

1 Place squash, cut side up, in large microwavable dish; cover with wax paper. Microwave on High until fork-tender, about 15 minutes. (Alternatively, to bake squash in oven, preheat oven to 400°F. Spray large rimmed baking sheet with nonstick spray. Place squash, cut side down, on baking sheet and bake until tender, 50 minutes.)

2 Meanwhile, to make picadillo, heat oil in large nonstick skillet over medium heat. Add onion and bell pepper; cook, stirring often, until vegetables are softened, 5 minutes. Stir in soy crumbles, chili powder, and cumin; cook, stirring often, 2 minutes.

3 Add water, tomato sauce, raisins, olives, vinegar, and Worcestershire sauce; bring to boil. Reduce heat and simmer, stirring occasionally, until slightly thickened, 8 minutes. Mound ¼ of picadillo evenly into one cooked squash half.

4 To serve, place one stuffed squash half on plate.

PER SERVING (1 squash half and 1¼ cups picadillo):
358 Cal, 7 g Total Fat, 0 g Sat Fat, 0 g Trans Fat, 0 mg Chol, 475 mg Sod, 50 g Carb, 21 g Sugar, 16 g Fib, 18 g Prot, 224 mg Calc.

8 PointsPlus® value

STORE AND SERVE LATER

Let the remaining squash and picadillo cool completely. Keeping squash and picadillo separate, place each into three separate airtight containers and cover. Refrigerate up to 4 days. To reheat one serving, transfer 1 squash half to a microwavable plate. Fill with ⅓ of picadillo. Cover with wax paper and microwave on High until heated through, about 2 minutes.

VEGGIE SHEPHERD'S PIES

SERVES 1 PLUS LEFTOVERS

2 teaspoons olive oil

▲ 2 carrots, sliced

▲ 2 cups chopped cauliflower

▲ 1 onion, chopped

▲ 1 red bell pepper, chopped

2 tablespoons all-purpose flour

▲ 1 cup reduced-sodium vegetable broth

▲ 1 cup canned cannellini (white kidney) beans, rinsed and drained

▲ ½ pound cremini mushrooms, quartered

2 tablespoons minced fresh thyme

2 tablespoons red-wine vinegar

¼ teaspoon salt

2 cups frozen shredded potatoes (unthawed)

¼ cup grated Parmesan cheese

1 Preheat oven to 400°F. Spray 4 (2-cup) baking dishes or ovenproof bowls with nonstick spray. (Alternatively, spray 9-inch square baking dish with nonstick spray.)

2 Heat oil in large saucepan over medium heat. Add carrots, cauliflower, onion, and bell pepper. Cook, stirring occasionally, until vegetables are softened, 5 minutes. Sprinkle vegetables with flour and stir to coat. Slowly add broth and cook, stirring constantly, until mixture comes to boil.

3 Add beans, mushrooms, thyme, vinegar, and salt; return to boil. Reduce heat and simmer until vegetables are tender, 3 minutes. Spoon into prepared baking dishes. Top evenly with potatoes; sprinkle potatoes with Parmesan. Place baking dishes on baking sheet and bake until filling is bubbling, about 20 minutes. (If using 9-inch baking dish, bake 35 minutes.) Let stand 5 minutes before serving.

PER SERVING (1 pie): 245 Cal, 4 g Total Fat, 1 g Sat Fat, 0 g Trans Fat, 4 mg Chol, 473 mg Sod, 43 g Carb, 9 g Sugar, 9 g Fib, 11 g Prot, 146 mg Calc.

STORE AND SERVE LATER

Let the remaining pies cool completely and cover. Refrigerate up to 4 days or freeze up to 4 months. To reheat one serving, if frozen, thaw in the refrigerator overnight. Cover with wax paper and microwave on High until heated through, about 2 minutes.

CHICKPEA, SWEET POTATO, AND GREENS STEW

SERVES 1   PLUS LEFTOVERS

1   **teaspoon olive oil**

▲ 1   **onion, chopped**

1   **tablespoon minced peeled fresh ginger**

1   **garlic clove, minced**

½   **teaspoon cinnamon**

½   **teaspoon ground cumin**

¼   **teaspoon cayenne**

¼   **teaspoon salt**

▲ 2½   **cups reduced-sodium vegetable broth**

▲ 2   **sweet potatoes (about 1½ pounds), peeled and cut into 1-inch chunks**

¼   **cup golden raisins**

1   **teaspoon honey**

▲ 1   **bunch Swiss chard (about ¾ pound), tough stems removed, leaves chopped**

▲ 1   **(15½-ounce) can chickpeas, rinsed and drained**

1 Heat oil in large saucepan over medium-high heat. Add onion and cook, stirring occasionally, until softened, 5 minutes. Add ginger, garlic, cinnamon, cumin, cayenne, and salt. Cook, stirring constantly, until fragrant, 1 minute.

2 Add broth, sweet potatoes, raisins, and honey; bring to boil. Reduce heat and simmer, covered, until vegetables are almost tender, 10 minutes.

3 Add Swiss chard and chickpeas to saucepan. Return to boil, stirring occasionally, until Swiss chard wilts. Reduce heat and simmer, covered, until vegetables are tender, about 10 minutes. To serve, ladle 1½ cups stew into bowl.

PER SERVING (1½ cups): 273 Cal, 3 g Total Fat, 0 g Sat Fat, 0 g Trans Fat, 0 mg Chol, 748 mg Sod, 57 g Carb, 16 g Sugar, 10 g Fib, 9 g Prot, 117 mg Calc.

STORE AND SERVE LATER

Let the remaining stew cool completely. Divide the stew among three airtight containers and cover. Refrigerate up to 4 days. To reheat one serving, transfer to a small saucepan. Cover and cook over medium heat, stirring occasionally, until heated through, about 5 minutes.

BLACK-AND-JACK CHILES RELLENOS

SERVES 1 PLUS LEFTOVERS

- ▲ 4 **large poblano peppers**
- ▲ 1 **(14½-ounce) can stewed tomatoes**
- ▲ 3 **scallions, chopped**
- 1 **teaspoon dried oregano**
- 1½ **teaspoons ground cumin**
- ⅛ **teaspoon cinnamon**
- ½ **teaspoon salt**
- ▲ 1½ **cups thawed frozen corn kernels**
- ▲ 1 **cup canned black beans, rinsed and drained**
- ▲ 1 **(8.8-ounce) package cooked brown rice (about 1¾ cups)**
- 2 **teaspoons chopped chipotles en adobo**
- ⅓ **cup chopped fresh cilantro**
- 1 **cup shredded reduced-fat Monterey Jack cheese**
- **Lime wedges**

1 To roast poblanos, preheat boiler. Line medium rimmed baking sheet with foil; place peppers on foil. Broil 5 inches from heat, turning often, until skins blister, about 10 minutes. Transfer peppers to counter and wrap in foil. Let stand 15 minutes. When cool enough to handle, peel blackened skin off peppers. Use sharp knife to make long slit in one side of each pepper; remove seeds and membranes, being careful not to tear peppers.

2 Preheat oven to 425°F. Spray same baking sheet with nonstick spray.

3 To make filling, combine tomatoes, scallions, oregano, cumin, cinnamon, and salt in blender or food processor; puree. Transfer to large skillet and cook over medium heat, stirring occasionally, until thickened slightly, 8 minutes. Stir in corn, beans, rice, and chipotles. Cook, stirring often, until heated through, about 2 minutes. Remove from heat. Stir in cilantro and ½ cup Monterey Jack. Spoon filling evenly into peppers; place on prepared baking sheet. Sprinkle peppers with remaining ½ cup cheese. Bake until cheese is melted, about 15 minutes.

4 To serve, transfer 1 stuffed pepper to plate; serve with lime wedges.

PER SERVING (1 stuffed pepper): 365 Cal, 8 g Total Fat, 4 g Sat Fat, 0 g Trans Fat, 15 mg Chol, 971 mg Sod, 58 g Carb, 4 g Sugar, 10 g Fib, 17 g Prot, 493 mg Calc.

9 PointsPlus value

STORE AND SERVE LATER

Let the remaining stuffed peppers cool completely. Divide the peppers among three airtight containers and cover. Refrigerate up to 4 days or freeze up to 4 months. To reheat one serving, if frozen, thaw in the refrigerator overnight. Transfer the pepper to a microwavable dish. Cover with wax paper and microwave on High until heated through, about 2 minutes.

Black beans and Monterey Jack cheese fill mildly spiced poblanos.
BLACK-AND-JACK CHILES RELLENOS

Refrigerated dough and frozen spinach make these easy to prepare.
SPINACH-BROCCOLI CALZONES

SPINACH-BROCCOLI CALZONES

SERVES 1 PLUS LEFTOVERS

▲ **1 cup finely chopped fresh broccoli**

2 shallots, chopped

▲ **1 (10-ounce) package frozen chopped spinach, thawed and squeezed dry**

1 cup part-skim ricotta

¼ cup shredded part-skim mozzarella

⅓ cup shredded provolone cheese

▲ **1 large egg**

1 teaspoon Italian seasoning

1 pound refrigerated whole wheat pizza dough

1 cup fat-free marinara sauce, heated

1 Preheat oven to 425°F. Spray large baking sheet with nonstick spray.

2 Place broccoli and shallots in medium microwavable bowl. Cover with wax paper and microwave on High until vegetables are softened, 1½ minutes. Transfer to large bowl and let cool slightly. Add spinach, ricotta, mozzarella, provolone, egg, and Italian seasoning. Stir to combine.

3 Sprinkle work surface lightly with flour. Place dough on surface; cut into 4 pieces. With lightly floured rolling pin, roll each piece of dough into 6 x 8-inch oval. Spoon one-fourth of spinach mixture over half of oval, leaving ¾-inch border. Fold dough lengthwise over filling, crimping edges to seal. Repeat with remaining dough and filling.

4 Transfer calzones to prepared baking sheet. Bake until golden brown, 22 minutes. Let cool 5 minutes. Serve with marinara sauce.

PER SERVING (1 calzone and ¼ cup sauce): 477 Cal, 12 g Total Fat, 5 g Sat Fat, 0 g Trans Fat, 82 mg Chol, 985 mg Sod, 63 g Carb, 1 g Sugar, 10 g Fib, 25 g Prot, 457 mg Calc.

STORE AND SERVE LATER

Let the remaining calzones cool completely and individually wrap. Refrigerate up to 4 days or freeze up to 4 months. To reheat one serving, if frozen, thaw in the refrigerator overnight. Preheat the oven to 425°F. Unwrap calzone and place on a baking sheet. Bake until heated through, about 15 minutes. Serve calzone with ¼ cup heated fat-free marinara sauce.

Recipes by *PointsPlus* value

Recipes that work with the Simply Filling technique

Index

Dry and Liquid Measurement Equivalents

If you are converting the recipes in this book to metric measurements, use the following chart as a guide.

TEASPOONS	TABLESPOONS	CUPS	FLUID OUNCES	VOLUME	
3 teaspoons	1 tablespoon		1/2 fluid ounce	1/4 teaspoon	1 milliliter
6 teaspoons	2 tablespoons	1/8 cup	1 fluid ounce	1/2 teaspoon	2 milliliters
8 teaspoons	2 tablespoons plus 2 teaspoons	1/6 cup		1 teaspoon	5 milliliters
12 teaspoons	4 tablespoons	1/4 cup	2 fluid ounces	1 tablespoon	15 milliliters
15 teaspoons	5 tablespoons	1/3 cup minus 1 teaspoon		2 tablespoons	30 milliliters
16 teaspoons	5 tablespoons plus 1 teaspoon	1/3 cup		3 tablespoons	45 milliliters
18 teaspoons	6 tablespoons	1/4 cup plus 2 tablespoons	3 fluid ounces	1/4 cup	60 milliliters
24 teaspoons	8 tablespoons	1/2 cup	4 fluid ounces	1/3 cup	80 milliliters
30 teaspoons	10 tablespoons	1/2 cup plus 2 tablespoons	5 fluid ounces	1/2 cup	120 milliliters
32 teaspoons	10 tablespoons plus 2 teaspoons	2/3 cup		2/3 cup	160 milliliters
36 teaspoons	12 tablespoons	3/4 cup	6 fluid ounces	3/4 cup	175 milliliters
42 teaspoons	14 tablespoons	1 cup minus 2 tablespoons	7 fluid ounces	1 cup	240 milliliters
45 teaspoons	15 tablespoons	1 cup minus 1 tablespoon		1 quart	950 milliliters
48 teaspoons	16 tablespoons	1 cup	8 fluid ounces	**LENGTH**	
				1 inch	25 millimeters

OVEN TEMPERATURE					
250°F	120°C	400°F	200°C	1 inch	2.5 centimeters
275°F	140°C	425°F	220°C	**WEIGHT**	
300°F	150°C	450°F	230°C	1 ounce	30 grams
325°F	160°C	475°F	250°C	1/4 pound	120 grams
350°F	180°C	500°F	260°C	1/2 pound	240 grams
375°F	190°C	525°F	270°C	1 pound	480 grams

Note: Measurement of less than 1/8 teaspoon is considered a dash or a pinch. Metric volume measurements are approximate.